GLOBAL VIEWPOINTS

W9-CVA-080

Alcohol

Margaret Haerens, Book Editor

362.292
ALC

GREENHAVEN PRESS
A part of Gale, Cengage Learning

GALE
CENGAGE Learning

Detroit • New York • San Francisco • New Haven, Conn • Waterville, Maine • London

Elizabeth Des Chenes, *Director, Publishing Solutions*

© 2012 Greenhaven Press, a part of Gale, Cengage Learning

Gale and Greenhaven Press are registered trademarks used herein under license.

For more information, contact:
Greenhaven Press
27500 Drake Rd.
Farmington Hills, MI 48331-3535
Or you can visit our Internet site at gale.cengage.com

For product information and technology assistance, contact us at

Gale Customer Support, 1-800-877-4253
For permission to use material from this text or product, submit all requests online at www.cengage.com/permissions

Further permissions questions can be emailed to permissionrequest@cengage.com

Articles in Greenhaven Press anthologies are often edited for length to meet page requirements. In addition, original titles of these works are changed to clearly present the main thesis and to explicitly indicate the author's opinion. Every effort is made to ensure that Greenhaven Press accurately reflects the original intent of the authors. Every effort has been made to trace the owners of copyrighted material.

LIBRARY OF CONGRESS CATALOGING-IN-PUBLICATION DATA

Alcohol / Margaret Haerens, book editor.
    p. cm. -- (Global viewpoints)
    Includes bibliographical references and index.
    ISBN 978-0-7377-5642-5 (hbk.) -- ISBN 978-0-7377-5643-2 (pbk.)
    1. Drinking of alcoholic beverages. 2. Alcoholism--Social aspects. I. Haerens, Margaret.
    HV5035.A42 2012
    362.292--dc23
                                                            2011047671

Printed in the United States of America
    1 2 3 4 5   16 15 14 13 12

ED156

Contents

Chapter 1: Trends in Alcohol Abuse

Alcohol consumption is a major health problem in many parts of the world, yet programs to address the issue remain a low priority in public policy. Heavy episodic drinking is particularly dangerous and has consequences not just for the individual, but for society.

Cheap legal liquor and illegal alcoholic beverages are contributing to substance abuse rates in Kenya. Health and government officials have urged the president to designate alcohol and drug abuse a national emergency.

Alcohol abuse is one of Australia's most serious problems, yet it is not being adequately addressed because alcohol consumption is integral to Australian culture. The Australian government needs to take meaningful measures to curb alcoholism and its effects.

There is a long tradition of drinking alcohol in Turkey. A recent study by the Green Crescent organization bemoans the tradition and asserts that it is responsible for a variety of Turkey's problems. Critics of the report point out that the rate of alcohol consumption in Turkey is moderate compared to most European countries.

Chapter 2: Strategies to Curb Alcohol Abuse

Chapter 3: Religion and Alcohol

Chapter 4: Alcohol Culture and Tradition

Foreword

"The problems of all of humanity can only be solved by all of humanity."
—Swiss author Friedrich Dürrenmatt

Global interdependence has become an undeniable reality. Mass media and technology have increased worldwide access to information and created a society of global citizens. Understanding and navigating this global community is a challenge, requiring a high degree of information literacy and a new level of learning sophistication.

Building on the success of its flagship series, Opposing Viewpoints, Greenhaven Press has created the Global Viewpoints series to examine a broad range of current, often controversial topics of worldwide importance from a variety of international perspectives. Providing students and other readers with the information they need to explore global connections and think critically about worldwide implications, each Global Viewpoints volume offers a panoramic view of a topic of widespread significance.

Drugs, famine, immigration—a broad, international treatment is essential to do justice to social, environmental, health, and political issues such as these. Junior high, high school, and early college students, as well as general readers, can all use Global Viewpoints anthologies to discern the complexities relating to each issue. Readers will be able to examine unique national perspectives while, at the same time, appreciating the interconnectedness that global priorities bring to all nations and cultures.

Material in each volume is selected from a diverse range of sources, including journals, magazines, newspapers, nonfiction books, speeches, government documents, pamphlets, organization newsletters, and position papers. Global Viewpoints is truly global, with material drawn primarily from international sources available in English and secondarily from US sources with extensive international coverage.

Features of each volume in the Global Viewpoints series include:

- An **annotated table of contents** that provides a brief summary of each essay in the volume, including the name of the country or area covered in the essay.

- An **introduction** specific to the volume topic.

- A **world map** to help readers locate the countries or areas covered in the essays.

- For each viewpoint, an **introduction** that contains notes about the author and source of the viewpoint explains why material from the specific country is being presented, summarizes the main points of the viewpoint, and offers three **guided reading questions** to aid in understanding and comprehension.

- **For further discussion** questions that promote critical thinking by asking the reader to compare and contrast aspects of the viewpoints or draw conclusions about perspectives and arguments.

- A worldwide list of **organizations to contact** for readers seeking additional information.

- A **periodical bibliography** for each chapter and a **bibliography of books** on the volume topic to aid in further research.

- A comprehensive **subject index** to offer access to people, places, events, and subjects cited in the text, with the countries covered in the viewpoints highlighted.

Global Viewpoints is designed for a broad spectrum of readers who want to learn more about current events, history, political science, government, international relations, economics, environmental science, world cultures, and sociology—students doing research for class assignments or debates, teachers and faculty seeking to supplement course materials, and others wanting to understand current issues better. By presenting how people in various countries perceive the root causes, current consequences, and proposed solutions to worldwide challenges, Global Viewpoints volumes offer readers opportunities to enhance their global awareness and their knowledge of cultures worldwide.

Introduction

"Alcoholic beverages are widely consumed throughout the world. While most of the adult population drinks at low-risk levels most of the time or abstains altogether, the broad range of alcohol consumption patterns, from daily heavy drinking to occasional hazardous drinking, creates significant public health and safety problems in nearly all countries."

—Global Status
Report on Alcohol and Health,
World Health Organization, 2011

The first evidence of alcoholic beverages can be traced back to ancient times, at least as early as the Neolithic period (around 10,000 BC). Some experts have posited that it was the Chinese who were the first to make alcohol in the form of a wine made by fermenting rice, honey, and fruit, as far back as 7000 BC. The prevalence of wild grape fields in the Middle East led winemakers in that region to ferment grapes to make rich, potent wines. Many of the wines from this era were made with fruit, berries, and honey. Wine quickly became an integral part of daily life in Mediterranean and Middle Eastern countries and was used widely for medicinal and religious purposes in many areas.

In Persia, or modern-day Iran, archaeologists discovered an earthen jug still filled with a yellow wine dating from 5500–5000 BC. In ancient Egypt, there is much evidence that wine, beer, and other forms of alcoholic beverages were essential parts of everyday existence: Most homes brewed their own beer; beer and wine were deified and offered as gifts to the gods; alcohol was valued as payment for services; and the dead were buried with jugs of wine and beer for the afterlife. The Egyptians revered Osiris, the god they credited with teaching them brewing. In ancient Greece, alcohol was a gift from Dionysius, the god of the grape. In Greece, as well as in the Roman Empire, alcohol played a central role in social and religious life.

Other cultures also developed their own alcohol tradition. Dating as far back as AD 200, the Mesoamerica people made *pulque*, a potent beverage fermented from maguey juice. The Mayans brewed a wine made from honey called *balché*. In Brazil, indigenous populations fermented maize or manioc with fruit to make *cauim*. The Iroquois utilized sap from the sugar maple tree to make alcohol in what today is America. In Africa, palm wine made of sorghum or millet played a key social role in many communities.

Distilled liquors were facilitated by the development of the distilling process, which existed in ancient times but was developed in the early centuries AD. By the Middle Ages, many of the liquors still popular today were created. For example, there are mentions of vodka in Poland and Russia as far back as the late ninth century, and historians have traced the first known vodka distillery to Khylnovsk, Russia, in AD 1174. In Ireland and Scotland, distillers used barley to make whiskey by the twelfth century. In the sixteenth century, Scandinavian countries were enjoying *akvavit*, a liquor traditionally spiced with caraway or dill.

As the technology for making alcoholic beverages advanced and enterprising men and women experimented with different ingredients and techniques, alcohol cemented its role as integral to social and religious life. It was accessible by all people, whether rich or poor, and was served at meals, festivals, dances, religious and political events, and holidays. Overindulgence was a regular occurrence. In many societies, alcohol was an everyday beverage to be enjoyed at all times of the day. However, it was always true that religious and sociocultural beliefs influenced drinking habits and alcohol culture in communities around the world. For example, the spread of Christianity led to a biblical interpretation of alcohol: In the Bible, wine is used and enjoyed in moderation, but to drink in excess is wrong. In Islam, alcoholic beverages are strictly *haram*, or forbidden.

With the advent of the early modern period, cultural attitudes toward alcoholic consumption began to shift. Once tolerant of drunkenness, many countries began to frown on overindulgence as undisciplined and dangerous. In early eighteenth-century Britain, cheap gin led to a "gin craze," an epidemic of extreme drunkenness and alcoholism that inspired a legislative backlash. The era of industrialization in the nineteenth century dictated the need for a reliable and efficient workforce, and soon temperance movements to curb excessive drinking were gaining influence in many Western countries.

The temperance movement in the United States managed to successfully advocate for the ratification of the Eighteenth Amendment to the US Constitution that called for a complete prohibition on the sale, manufacture, and transportation of alcohol from 1920 to 1933. This time period came to be known as the Prohibition Era. The law proved profoundly unpopular with the American people and spurred the spread of organized crime, which ran moonshine and bootlegged liquor to underground drinking establishments. In rural areas, bootleggers and moonshiners supplied communities with liquor. The US experiment with prohibition was a failure, and the Eighteenth Amendment was repealed in 1933.

As long as alcohol has been around, so has been the problem of excessive drinking and alcoholism. There are many accounts throughout history of overindulgence, but accurate records were not kept as to the health problems, physical and societal damage, and alcohol-fueled violence witnessed as a result of drunkenness. Addictions to alcohol were treated privately and widespread records of such efforts were not kept.

As medicine and psychology developed, however, physicians began to confront the problem. In 1849 Swedish physician Magnus Huss first coined the term "alcoholism" to describe an alcohol addiction. In 1935 the Alcoholics Anonymous movement was born in an attempt to bring alcoholics together to remain sober and help others in the same condition. That same year, the US government opened the first alcohol treatment center in Lexington, Kentucky. In the years that followed, drug and alcohol rehabilitation centers became an effective and popular way to treat addictions.

Today, there is a deep understanding of the benefits and dangers to alcohol consumption. In his "History of Alcohol and Drinking Around the World," author David J. Hanson regards alcohol to be a benefit to humans over time. "Alcohol is a product that has provided a variety of functions for people throughout all history," he observes. "From the earliest times to the present, alcohol has played an important role in religion and worship. Historically, alcoholic beverages have served as sources of needed nutrients and have been widely used for their medicinal, antiseptic, and analgesic properties. The role of such beverages as thirst quenchers is obvious, and they play an important role in enhancing the enjoyment and quality of life. They can be a social lubricant, can facilitate relaxation, can provide pharmacological pleasure, and can increase the pleasure of eating. Thus, while alcohol has always been misused by a minority of drinkers, it has proved to be beneficial to most."

The authors of the viewpoints in *Global Viewpoints: Alcohol* explore many of these issues: the role alcohol plays in culture and tradition, the relationship between religion and alcohol, alcohol consumption trends, and strategies to curb alcoholism and excessive drinking. The information in this volume provides insight into ways governments around the world are attempting to balance consumer rights and individual freedom with the public health problems of alcohol addiction, alcohol-fueled violence, underage drinking, and dangerous homemade and illegal liquor.

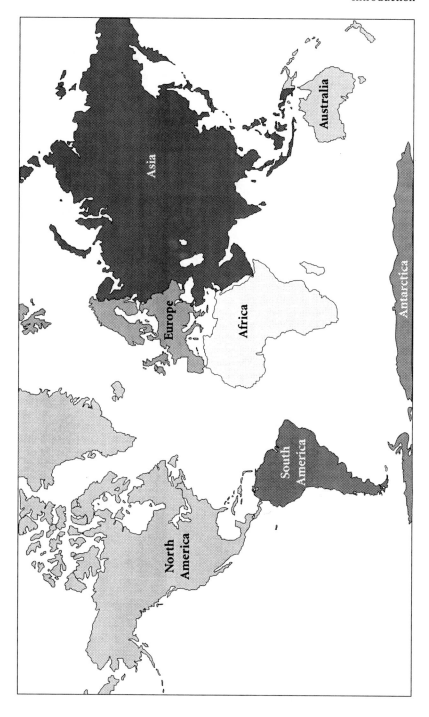

Trends in Alcohol Abuse

Global Trends in Alcohol Consumption

World Health Organization

The World Health Organization (WHO) is the United Nations agency that focuses on international health policy. In the following viewpoint, WHO officials cite alcohol abuse as a major contributing factor to death, disease, and injury around the world and contend that it holds a grave cost to communities and societies. However, addressing the problem is a low public health priority in many countries. Formulating stronger and more effective policies to reduce the health, safety, and socioeconomic costs of alcohol abuse should be essential for global, national, and local public health officials.

As you read, consider the following questions:

1. According to WHO, how many deaths does alcohol contribute to every year?
2. In how many types of diseases and injuries does WHO assert that alcohol plays a factor?
3. How many countries have adopted some type of formal policies on alcohol since 1999, according to WHO?

The public health objective on alcohol of the World Health Organization (WHO) is to reduce the health burden caused by the harmful use of alcohol and, thereby, to save

World Health Organization, "Introduction," *Global Status Report on Alcohol and Health*, who.int, 2011, pp. x–xii. Reprinted by permission.

lives, reduce disease and prevent injuries. The hazardous and harmful use of alcohol is a major global contributing factor to death, disease and injury: to the drinker through health impacts, such as alcohol dependence, liver cirrhosis, cancers and injuries; and to others through the dangerous actions of intoxicated people, such as drink-driving and violence, or through the impact of drinking on fetus and child development. The harmful use of alcohol results in approximately 2.5 million deaths each year, with a net loss of life of 2.25 million, taking into account the estimated beneficial impact of low levels of alcohol use on some diseases in some population groups. Harmful drinking can also be very costly to communities and societies. . . .

Alcohol consumption and problems related to alcohol vary widely around the world, but the burden of disease and death remains significant in most countries.

A Dire Threat

Alcohol consumption and problems related to alcohol vary widely around the world, but the burden of disease and death remains significant in most countries. Alcohol consumption is the world's third largest risk factor for disease and disability; in middle-income countries, it is the greatest risk. Alcohol is a causal factor in 60 types of diseases and injuries and a component cause in 200 others. Almost 4% of all deaths worldwide are attributed to alcohol, greater than deaths caused by HIV/AIDS, violence or tuberculosis. Alcohol is also associated with many serious social issues, including violence, child neglect and abuse, and absenteeism in the workplace.

Yet, despite all these problems, the harmful use of alcohol remains a low priority in public policy, including in health policy. Many lesser health risks have higher priority.

Who Is Most at Risk?

The harmful use of alcohol is a particularly grave threat to men. It is the leading risk factor for death in males ages 15–59, mainly due to injuries, violence and cardiovascular diseases. Globally, 6.2% of all male deaths are attributable to alcohol, compared to 1.1% of female deaths. Men also have far greater rates of total burden attributed to alcohol than women—7.4% for men compared to 1.4% for women. Men outnumber women four to one in weekly episodes of heavy drinking—most probably the reason for their higher death and disability rates. Men also have much lower rates of abstinence compared to women. Lower socioeconomic status and educational levels result in a greater risk of alcohol-related death, disease and injury—a social determinant that is greater for men than women.

Consumption Trends

The world's highest alcohol consumption levels are found in the developed world, including western and eastern Europe. High-income countries generally have the highest alcohol consumption. However, it does not follow that high income and high consumption always translate into high alcohol-related problems and high-risk drinking. Western European countries have some of the highest consumption rates but their net alcohol-attributable mortality rates are relatively low, though their alcohol-related disease burden may be high. Many eastern European countries have the highest consumption, risky patterns of drinking and, accordingly, high levels of alcohol-related deaths and disabilities. Every fifth death is due to harmful drinking in the Commonwealth of Independent States (CIS). Outside of the Russian Federation and some neighbouring countries, rates of disease and disability attributable to alcohol are also quite high, for example, in Mexico and in most South American countries.

Figure 1. Total adult (15+) per capita consumption, in litres of pure alcohol, 2005[a]

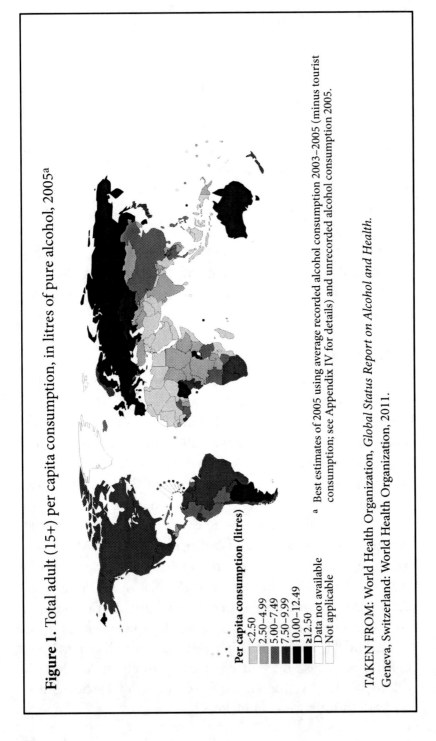

Per capita consumption (litres)
- <2.50
- 2.50–4.99
- 5.00–7.49
- 7.50–9.99
- 10.00–12.49
- ≥12.50
- Data not available
- Not applicable

[a] Best estimates of 2005 using average recorded alcohol consumption 2003–2005 (minus tourist consumption; see Appendix IV for details) and unrecorded alcohol consumption 2005.

TAKEN FROM: World Health Organization, *Global Status Report on Alcohol and Health.* Geneva, Switzerland: World Health Organization, 2011.

Worldwide consumption in 2005 was equal to 6.13 litres of pure alcohol consumed per person aged 15 years or older. A large portion of this consumption—28.6% or 1.76 litres per person—was homemade, illegally produced or sold outside normal government controls. However, despite widespread consumption, a higher percentage of people currently do not drink at all. Almost half of all men and two-thirds of women have not consumed alcohol in the past year. Abstention rates are low in high-income, high-consumption countries, and higher in North African and South Asian countries with large Muslim populations. Female abstention rates are very high in these countries. Abstention from alcohol is very important in the global picture on alcohol consumption; it is one of the strongest predictors of the magnitude of alcohol-attributable burden of disease and injuries in populations. Obviously, lifetime abstention from alcohol means exemption from personal alcohol-attributable disease, injury and death. Because abstention is so prevalent in the world, any diminution in abstention trends could have a big impact on the global burden of disease caused by the harmful use of alcohol.

The Problem of Heavy Drinking

Heavy episodic drinking is another important pattern of drinking because it leads to serious health problems, and is particularly associated with injury. About 11.5% of drinkers have heavy episodic drinking occasions. Heavy episodic drinking is not the only measure of harmful drinking, but data for this aspect of the drinking pattern were not available in many countries. The pattern of drinking score, reflecting the frequency and circumstances of alcohol consumption and the proportion of people drinking alcohol to intoxication, is among the lowest, i.e., less risky, in western European countries, while it is the highest in the Russian Federation, and in some neighbouring countries. Risky patterns of drinking are also highly prevalent in Mexico and southern African countries.

Harmful alcohol consumption is risky both for the drinker and for other people. An intoxicated person can put people in harm's way by involving them in traffic accidents or violent behaviour, or by negatively affecting co-workers, relatives, friends or strangers. A survey in Australia found that two-thirds of respondents were adversely affected by someone else's drinking in the past year. Alcohol consumption also affects society at large. Death, disease and injury caused by alcohol consumption have socioeconomic impacts, including the medical costs borne by governments, and the financial and psychological burden to families. The hazardous and harmful use of alcohol also impacts on workers' productivity. Perhaps the biggest social impact is crime and violence related to alcohol consumption, which create significant costs for justice and law enforcement sectors.

Contrary to the belief of many people, the health, safety and socioeconomic problems attributable to alcohol can be effectively reduced.

Confronting the Problem

Contrary to the belief of many people, the health, safety and socioeconomic problems attributable to alcohol can be effectively reduced. Many evidence-based alcohol policies and prevention programmes are shown to work. One of the most effective is raising alcohol prices by raising taxes. This has the added benefit of generating increased revenues. A recent analysis of 112 studies on the effects of alcohol tax increases affirmed that when taxes go up, drinking goes down, including among problem drinkers and youth. Implementing and enforcing legal drinking ages for the purchase and consumption of alcohol is another effective way to reduce alcohol-attributable problems, as is the setting of maximum blood alcohol concentrations (BACs) for drivers and enforcing them with sobriety checkpoints and random breath testing. These are effective and cost-effective ways to reduce alcohol-related traffic accidents.

Yet, not enough countries use these and other effective policy options to prevent death, disease and injury attributable to alcohol consumption. Since 1999, when WHO first began to report on alcohol policies, at least 34 countries have adopted some type of formal policies. Restrictions on alcohol marketing and on drink-driving have increased but, in general, there are no clear trends on most preventive measures. A large proportion of countries, representing a high percentage of the global population, has weak alcohol policies and prevention programmes that do not protect the health and safety of the populace.

Kenya Deems Alcohol Abuse a National Disgrace

Irene Mwivano

Irene Mwivano is a reporter for Global Press Institute. In the following viewpoint, she maintains that Kenya's rising drug and alcohol addiction problem is being fostered by ineffective law enforcement and weak government policies. Government officials are being pressured by health officials and activists to deem the crisis a national emergency. Mwivano reports that cheap liquor and illegal alcohol are widely available, driving high rates of addiction. She asserts that the government should do a better job of providing information about treatment and rehabilitation services to Kenyans suffering from alcohol addiction.

As you read, consider the following questions:

1. How does the author describe "kujitibu"?

2. According to a 2007 government survey, what are the most commonly abused drugs in Kenya?

3. How many Kenyans in the 2007 government survey reported that they were not aware of any treatment or rehabilitation services in their area?

James Mwangi, 40, says alcohol allows him to escape from the hardships of his daily life. In fact, he says, drinking gets him through his workdays.

Irene Mwivano, "Rising Alcohol and Drug Abuse Becoming a National Emergency in Kenya," globalpressinstitute.org, February 10, 2011. Reprinted by permission.

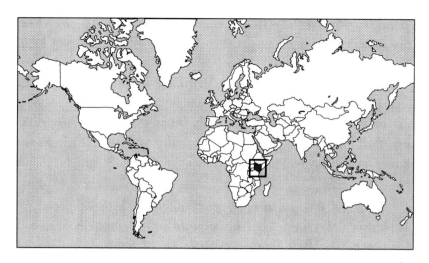

Today, he refills his bottle before staggering away to get back to work in a local Nairobi street market, where he peddles electronics and carries vegetables for merchants at the local market with his handcart.

Squeezed into narrow alleys throughout Nairobi, small kiosks sell cheap legal liquor and other illegal concoctions, like chang'aa, a traditional alcoholic beverage [whose] name translates to "kill me quick" for its use of dangerous substances such as jet fuel or embalming fluid. There are dozens of Kenyans, like Mwangi, who pop in and out of these kiosks every time they earn enough to afford a refill.

For Mwangi, refills of Kane Extra, a potent but legal brand of alcohol, sell for as little as 10 shillings, 12 cents USD [US dollar].

The "Kujitibu" Trend

Merchants say men and women between the ages of 15 and 60 frequent the kiosks multiple times each day, beginning as early as 8 a.m. for what they call "kujitibu." Kujitibu refers to drinking the measured doses of liquor necessary to maintain one's level of intoxication for as long as one's body can withstand. Customers say frequent stops at the kiosks give them the energy they need to get through their "backbreaking jobs" in the oppressive heat.

Mwangi says he has been drinking during work for the last 15 years. He says in that time he has seen many people die or end up in mental hospitals because of excessive drinking. Still, he says he has no plans to stop visiting the kiosks for liquor every day.

Squeezed into narrow alleys throughout Nairobi, small kiosks sell cheap legal liquor and other illegal concoctions, like chang'aa, a traditional alcoholic beverage [whose] name translates to "kill me quick" for its use of dangerous substances such as jet fuel or embalming fluid.

A National Crisis

Concern about drug and alcohol abuse in Kenya has grown in recent years, leading some to demand that the president and prime minister declare substance abuse a national disaster. Rehabilitation centers do exist, but many say they are expensive and inefficient, or they don't know where they are. The government has made new efforts to regulate drugs and alcohol, but advocates say corruption and ineffective law enforcement will continue to foster addiction here.

Last November [2010], Sheikh Mohamed Dor, a member of Parliament, MP, and the National Campaign Against Drug Abuse, NACADA, urged Kenyan President Mwai Kibaki and Prime Minister Raila Odinga to declare drug abuse a national disaster in Kenya. Their requests came just days before WikiLeaks, an international nonprofit organization that publishes secret documents, released a 2006 report by former U.S. Ambassador William Bellamy accusing Kenyan authorities of protecting drug lords and cartels. The Kenyan government called the accusations malicious and said the U.S. government had apologized.

Just days later, Michael Ranneberger, U.S. ambassador, announced that four senior Kenyan government officials and one businessman suspected of drug trafficking were barred from visiting the United States, as part of a group of U.S. initiatives to combat the drug trade in Kenya. Kenyan police investigated the group, former assistant minister and MP Harun Mwau, MP Hassan Joho, MP Gidion Mbuvi, MP William Kabogo and prominent businessman Ali Punjani. Two weeks ago [early 2011] police concluded there was not sufficient evidence to prosecute the group, according to the *Daily Nation*. The sequence of events has increased international awareness of drug and alcohol problems in Kenya.

A Widespread Problem

Dr. Frank Njenga, NACADA chairman, warns that Kenyans are dying in record numbers thanks to drug addiction and substance abuse. Njenga's announcement came after his agency released a report that revealed one in five adults in "hot spots" throughout the country used hard drugs.

According to the NACADA report, the most commonly used substance in Coast Province is alcohol, followed by miraa, a drug also known as khat—a plant that causes "euphoria" when chewed. Among other drugs, cannabis is the most used, followed by heroin and cocaine. Twelve percent of children ages 12 to 17 were already reported to be active users of alcohol and other substances, while they were found to be more likely to use cannabis and miraa than alcohol.

NACADA most recent survey of Kenyans, conducted in 2007, reported that substance abuse is a major social problem in Kenya. According to the survey, the most commonly abused drugs in Kenya are alcohol and tobacco. In the years since the survey, usage has continued to increase, Njenga says.

Drug Abuse

For substances other than alcohol, 13 percent of respondents ages 10 to 14 and almost half of respondents ages 15 to 65 reported having tried them. In both groups, more than double the number of males than females reported trying them. About 22 percent of respondents ages 15 to 65 said they were current users of at least one substance other than alcohol.

When it comes to abuse of drugs or alcohol, more than 60 percent of abusers reside in urban areas and 21 percent in rural areas, according to the survey. Young adults have the highest abuse prevalence, with Kenyans ages 10 to 19 accounting for half of drug abusers.

Origins of the Crisis

According to the former chairman of NACADA, Joseph Kaguthi, Kenya's drug problem began when the country was a transit route for hard drugs. According to the 2010 "International Narcotics Control Strategy Report," INCSR, Kenya is a significant transit country for cocaine, heroin and khat. An increased quantity of heroin and hashish has begun moving through Kenya from southwest Asia to Europe or the United States in recent years, while domestic heroin and cocaine production markets have also grown.

Kaguthi says that although hard drugs have gained a foothold in Kenya, alcohol and cigarettes remain the country's biggest problems, contributing to the disintegration of health and families.

The NACADA survey on Kenya reported that nearly 90 percent of cocaine and heroin users, 44 percent of bhang [an intoxicant derived from cannabis] users, and almost 40 percent of tobacco and alcohol users said that they had diverted resources meant for domestic use to buy drugs during the year before the survey. The survey added that drug and substance abusers are less economically productive, citing absenteeism from school and work, crime and violence.

The Popularity of Chang'aa

So common is chang'aa [a traditional alcoholic beverage] across the Kenyan countryside that some policy makers say regulating it may make more sense than driving it further underground. Homemade liquor plays a central role in many cultural ceremonies, and the government has generally allowed chang'aa to be ladled out for that purpose.

Marc Lacey,
"A Poor Man's Solace Once Again Delivers a Deadly Blow,"
New York Times, July 7, 2005.

According to the survey, substance abuse in Kenya is the result of optimal market conditions, including poor law enforcement, weak policies, unemployment, poverty, corruption and the breakdown of traditional values.

Consequences of Drug and Alcohol Abuse

Drug and alcohol abuse in Kenya has also led to an increase in related social, medical and economic problems, including poor health, domestic violence, reduced productivity, increased crime, sexual violence, unsafe sex and exposure to HIV/AIDS.

Mwangi says some addicts seek help at local rehabilitation centers.

Drug and alcohol abuse in Kenya has also led to an increase in related social, medical and economic problems, including poor health, domestic violence, reduced productivity, increased crime, sexual violence, unsafe sex and exposure to HIV/AIDS.

The most common rehabilitation facility is Kenyatta National Hospital Support Centre and Rehabilitation Services, says Dr. Muhammad Mahmud Swale, one of its doctors.

"My work and that of my team is to bring back young people from the brinks of self-destruction through alcohol and drug abuse by offering them in-patient counseling," Swale says.

Treatment Options

In all, there are 41 rehabilitation centers recognized by NACADA that treat more than 1,000 patients a day. Kenyatta charges patients between 200 shillings, $2.50 USD, and 350 shillings, $4 USD, a cost that is prohibitive for many like Mwangi, among the half of the population who lives below the poverty line.

A cheaper rehab option is often found at Mathare Psychiatric Hospital, a government facility, which is less expensive than private centers, Swale says. But a lack of space forces addicts to wait as long as three months for entry.

Patients also say local rehab centers are uncoordinated and unregulated, lacking standards and guidelines.

"Just like other fields, there has been a problem with the standards," Njenga says. "There are people who even operate from their sitting rooms and claim to be offering rehabilitation services. But we are in the process of setting up standards."

Improving Treatment

Local authorities have determined minimum standards for residential rehab facilities and programs to ensure professionalism. The guidelines seek to protect clients from exploitation by ensuring that they get the services they pay for and to establish a system to mobilize resources and medical insurance coverage.

Raising Awareness

But the primary challenge in increasing participation in rehab facilities is awareness. Although the majority of respondents in the NACADA survey of Coast Province agreed that drug addicts should be taken into rehabilitation facilities, only 14 percent knew of any facilities in their communities or regions. More than 60 percent of the respondents in the survey of all of Kenya said they were not aware of the available treatment and rehabilitation services.

Other Ways to Fight Addiction

Although the majority of Kenyans said they were in favor of restrictions on the sale of alcohol, new laws implemented in December [2010] created a fury of disapproval from local business owners.

Prevention of illegal drug use remains a larger problem.

Ranneberger says the substantial increase in drug trafficking in recent years threatens to impede economic growth in Kenya, erode its social fabric and undermine its hard-fought constitution, which was signed into law in August.

But both the INCSR and Ranneberger acknowledge that Kenya has also made progress in its fight against drug and substance abuse. In addition to its recent surveys, NACADA developed the National Strategy on Prevention, Control and Mitigation of Drug and Substance Abuse, 2009–2014, in 2009, as well as a National Action Plan on Drugs and Substance Abuse.

The number of trafficking arrests jumped from 67 in 2008 to 194 in 2009, while the amount of heroin seized in the same period grew from 3.7 kilograms of heroin to 8.5 kilograms and 2 kilograms of cocaine to 9 kilograms, according to the INCSR. According to the unit's statistics, police intercepted and seized around 350 million shillings, or $4.3 million USD, worth of drugs, mainly bhang.

According to the latest police records, overall crimes related to dangerous drugs decreased from 2009 to 2010. But although crimes of possession and handling decreased, trafficking and usage crimes more than doubled.

Australia Has a Severe Alcohol Abuse Problem

Nick Crofts

Nick Crofts is the director of Turning Point Alcohol & Drug Centre in Melbourne, Australia. In the following viewpoint, he states that Australia's alcohol problem is a national disgrace and that not enough is being done to address the crisis. He reports that alcohol abuse is ranked second only to tobacco on the scale of preventable causes of death in the country. Crofts contends that there needs to be more public awareness of the issue as well as a meaningful debate on how to fight alcohol abuse in Australia.

As you read, consider the following questions:

1. According to Crofts, how many Australians will be admitted to a hospital every day because of alcohol problems?
2. How many liters of beer does Crofts report an Australian drinks on average every year?
3. How many Australians are diagnosed with alcohol-related brain damage every year, according to the author?

Today about 175 Australians will go into hospital because of a major drug problem. After tobacco, it is the major drug problem in Australia, and one that we are not adequately

Nick Crofts, "This Country's Biggest Drug Problem Is Alcohol," www.theaustralian.com.au, February 24, 2007. Reprinted by permission.

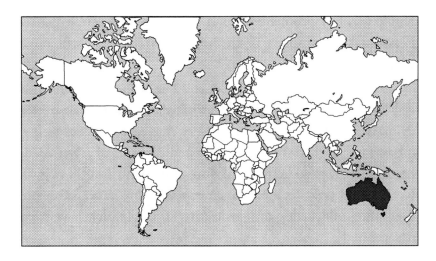

tackling—alcohol. It's also implicated in around 50 per cent of Australia's domestic and sexual assaults, and a major cause of imprisonment.

Australia, in fact, now has three major drug problems that urgently need to be tackled. They are alcohol, alcohol, and, of course, alcohol. And 175 Australians will be admitted to hospital because of this drug every single day of the year.

A National Disgrace

There is so much talk about being tough on drugs. Yet we are not tough on the one drug whose harm outweighs all the others put together—alcohol. It is not being addressed because our community simply accepts the effects of alcohol and the massive damage it is doing. We have allowed the fact that alcohol consumption trends have been more or less stable in Australia to lull us into taking for granted the huge burden of disease that is linked to alcohol—far beyond any impact that illicit drugs are having.

It is really a national disgrace. The *National Alcohol Strategy [2006–2009]* lays out the massive scope of Australia's problems with this drug: addiction, injuries, assaults, damage to family life, lost productivity, and chronic health problems. Yet if you ask Australians if alcohol is a drug, they will most probably say no.

It's estimated that in the past 12 months we drank our way through $23 billion worth of alcohol, and our desire for drink is unslakable. Every year, every Australian is consuming, on average, about 90 litres of beer and 22 litres of wine. Alcohol is a drug, is addictive, and does affect your health. It is, in fact, second only to tobacco as a preventable cause of death, even after subtracting any protective effects (which have been exaggerated).

It is estimated that 65,000 people are hospitalised annually as a result of their alcohol intake. High blood alcohol levels are a factor in a third of all road accident deaths, and in hundreds of thousands more cases where people are crippled but not killed.

Alcohol and Violence

Alcohol also has a strong connection with violence: Any police officer can tell you that at least half of those committing serious assaults are intoxicated. Studies find that there are more assaults around large clusters of pubs and licensed premises.

Also, why aren't we as a community talking about the issue of alcohol and brain damage? Many studies have shown strong and clear links between heavy drinking and brain damage. About 2,500 Australians are being diagnosed with alcohol-related brain damage every year. The longer the person drinks, the more likely they will be affected, and the damage is irreparable.

Alcohol-related brain damage has many adverse effects, including mood changes, confusion, issues with short-term memory, vision problems and cognitive difficulties. Yet there is no meaningful debate on a national level about this topic.

A Drunken Culture?

- A reputation for heavy drinking has been part of white Australia's national myth from rum corps during initial British colonisation, to drunkenness in the gold diggings, to the lasting traditions of bush workers' "shouts" and the end of week "work and burst" drunken blowouts.

- Today, more than one-third (35.4 percent) of the Australian population consumes alcohol at levels that are risky or a high risk for harm in the short-term at least once a year.

- Almost two-thirds (62.3 percent) of all alcohol in Australia is consumed at levels that are risky or a high risk for short-term harm.

Ministerial Council on Drug Strategy,
National Alcohol Strategy 2006–2009:
Towards Safer Drinking Cultures, *May 2006.*

The Effects of Alcohol

Many Australians do not realise the real effects of alcohol. A classic example of this is the issue of alcohol and cancer. Alcohol substantially increases the risk of cancer, including cancer of the mouth, liver and breast. Yet a survey by Roy Morgan Research in September last year [2006] revealed 61 per cent of those surveyed were unaware of the link. The federal government needs to compel alcohol products to carry clear warnings. Australian wine bottled for export to the US carries a warning label, for instance with clear warnings about the dangers of mixing alcohol with pregnancy, yet Australian consumers can buy the same wine with no warnings.

Some countries, such as the US and India, have warning labels on bottles. Others, such as Sweden, have a series of warning messages on advertisements. The European Commission is looking at the issue, and so should we.

Alcohol has been shown to be causally related to more than 60 different medical conditions. The long-term risks of alcohol include brain and liver damage, heart disease, stroke, high blood pressure, cancers, stomach ulcers and the loss of sexual functions in men as well as infertility in women.

As for the health benefits from drinking, evidence suggests that light drinking on a regular basis benefits the heart of men over 40 and women past menopause—not of younger people. But this protective effect comes nowhere near balancing the number of years of life lost from the harms of drinking. The balance of alcohol's effect on health is overwhelmingly negative.

Alcohol is our big drug problem, the major drug scourge of Australia.

Confronting the Crisis

There are things that we know work to reduce the harm from alcohol. One is tax. Just as with cigarettes, if taxes are raised, people tend to buy and consume less—and the rates of alcohol-related problems go down. As a start, we need to tax drinks according to the amount of alcohol they contain. The current system lacks logic—you are currently often paying more tax to buy alcohol with less potency. For instance, one standard drink (containing about 10g of alcohol) of low-strength beer, with a 2.5 per cent alcohol content, may cost the consumer 22 cents in tax; for a standard drink of cask wine, however, with about 11 per cent alcohol, consumers pay just 7 cents.

Another way to reduce the harm is to limit the number of places where it is sold. Australia has too many liquor outlets, and alcohol is becoming easier than ever to purchase.

Turning Point [a treatment facility in Australia] is not anti-alcohol, but we are deeply alarmed about the lack of debate on this drug. The debate needs to start now, about the damage it's causing to the workplace, to our health, to young lives and the huge health and social problems it causes.

Alcohol is our big drug problem, the major drug scourge of Australia.

When will we wake up?

Turkey's Strong Tradition of Drinking Has Aroused Concerns About Abuse

Fazile Zahir

Fazile Zahir is a Turkish journalist. In the following viewpoint, she reports that escalating sales and consumption of alcohol in Turkey have prompted concerns from Islamic organizations about the country's alcohol problem. Unlike many Islamic countries, it is socially acceptable to drink in Turkey, and alcohol is widely available. Zahir also points to the country's strong tradition of alcohol drinking and argues that recent attempts by the ruling party to curb alcohol consumption and regulate alcohol sales have been largely ineffective.

As you read, consider the following questions:

1. According to Turkey's Green Crescent organization, how much is spent on alcohol every year in Turkey?

2. How many liters of beer does a Turk drink every year on average, according to the Green Crescent report?

3. According to the Tobacco and Alcohol Marketing Regulatory Agency, how much did volume sales of alcohol rise in 2008?

Fazile Zahir, "Turkey's Beer-Swillers Get Hammered," www.atimes.com, August 26, 2009. Reprinted by permission.

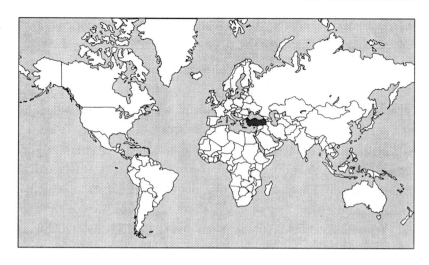

Turkey's Green Crescent (Yesil Ay) anti-alcohol, anti-tobacco organization produced a report on August 12 [2009] that indicated they believe the country is sinking into a barley-filled vat of iniquity.

According to their figures, the annual amount spent on alcohol has reached US$3.3 billion and consumption of wine, raki [a Turkish liquor] and spirits is rising. The report underlined the alarming nature of this trend by reminding the press and public that "85% of murders in Turkey, 50% of rapes, 50% of violent incidents, 65% of traffic accidents and 60% of all mental illnesses have alcohol as their root cause". Alcohol, the teetotallers point out, causes memory loss, blindness, stomach bleeding, heart problems and erectile dysfunction.

Green Crescent claims beer is the worst because it is the most widely consumed beverage. Turks now consume 15.4 liters per person each year. This figure, however, doesn't take into account how much is taken in by visiting tourists. And though it may be the highest level of consumption in the Muslim Middle East, when compared with 2004 figures such as 156.9 liters in Czechoslovakia, 131.1 liters in Ireland or 115.8 liters in Germany—it still looks very moderate.

European vs. Turkish Patterns of Alcohol Consumption

Perhaps one of the greatest cultural differences between European and Turkish patterns of alcohol consumption is the practice of abstinence among women. A March 2009 study on moderate and heavy alcohol consumption among Turks by the Turkish [Society] of Cardiology noted, "Light drinkers consisted of 294 men and 56 women, moderate drinkers of 215 men and 12 women, heavy drinkers of 88 men and five women and abstainers of 1,111 men and 1,662 women".

The study, which monitored 3,443 individuals for nine years, found that 2,773 never drank at all. Of the 19.5% who did drink, the majority of these—10.2%—were classed as light drinkers, 6.6% as moderate drinkers and only a tiny proportion, 2.7%, or 98 people, were classed as heavy drinkers.

Alcohol consumption is socially acceptable across most of Turkey. Even in conservative areas it is available in bars and shops where most patrons are male.

With a young and increasingly urban population, it's likely that demand for beer will continue its upward rise.

Raki Is Traditional

The traditional Turkish drink is raki, a strong aniseed-based spirit that is diluted with water and ice. In larger urban areas, young city dwellers go to bars just to drink, but it is far more common across Turkey to drink when one is eating as well. A hors d'oeuvre assortment is often referred to as a "raki table". Foods strongly associated with raki are fish, melon and white cheese.

Other Alcohol

Turkey is thought to be the first place in the world where wine was made, and even today it produces quality wines. The

Some Notes on Raki

Raki (rah-KUH) is similar to Greek ouzo and French pastis. When mixed with ice and/or water for drinking, it turns milky white. Because of its color and alcoholic punch, Turks call it lion's milk (aslan sütü).

Stacie Leone,
"Raki & Meze Simply Go Together,"
DEIK (Foreign Economic Relations Board). www.turkey-now.org.

largest domestic producers are Doluca and Kavaklidere and new popular wines have recently started to emerge from the Cappadocia and Aegean regions. (Although recently winemakers have complained of a heavy tax burden and a government they feel is unsympathetic to the wine industry due to its Islamist roots.)

The largest beer producer is Efes Pilsener, which dominates the market with an 80% market share. The ban on advertising alcohol means Efes is likely to remain on top for many years to come. In 2008, according to the Tobacco and Alcohol Market Regulatory [Authority], volume sales of alcohol rose by 19.5% and beer accounted for 9.5% of this rise.

With a young and increasingly urban population, it's likely that demand for beer will continue its upward rise. Efes has developed new light and dark beer brands over the past decade to capture an even larger market share and to help shape more sophisticated drinking habits.

Unlike the wine industry, beer producers have not complained of unwanted government interference and a recent excise rise was only to 9%—less than the national rate of inflation.

Alcohol in Turkey: A History

The tradition of drinking alcohol in Turkey is nothing new. James Caulfeild, the first earl of Charlemont who toured Turkey in the 1700s, observed, "The Turks are the soberest people on Earth yet some of them are apt to consider the words of the prophet in the literal sense and imagine if they abstain from the juice of the grape, they may drink any other spirituous liquor."

During the Ottoman era, alcohol fermentation and consumption were technically banned for Muslims. Still, the following tale is likely to be more than just an urban legend.

Sultan Murad the Fourth (1623–1640) was a heavy drinker, but imposed strict penalties for those found guilty of tobacco and alcohol consumption in his empire. He reputedly patrolled the streets of Istanbul in disguise and had drunks executed on the spot. During a raid on a secret wine cellar, he demanded to know why the vintner was flouting his prohibition. The winemaker replied, "Sultan, we put the grape juice in the barrel, but only God knows whether it becomes wine or vinegar."

In reality, wine making continued with little interference from the Ottoman authorities for 800 years. When the modern republic was established in 1923, wine and spirit making was nationalized under a state monopoly.

Islamic Crackdown on Alcohol

In recent years, the moderate Islamic ruling Justice and Development Party (AKP) has made several attempts to curb alcohol consumption through legislation and strict controls on establishments serving alcohol.

Since 2005, AKP mayors in Ankara [the capital of Turkey] have banned alcohol in government cafes and restaurants, citing the need to protect family values. New sales licenses have become harder to receive and extensions to existing permits are tied up in interminable bureaucratic delays.

In 2008, new legislation was passed that banned the sale of alcoholic drinks and cigarettes if the packaging was broken or divided (it was common in small shops to sell individual cigarettes). Some said this would be the end of selling wine by the glass in restaurants and bars, which accounts for around 35% of all wine consumed and that it would be impossible to make cocktails.

As of today [August 2009], the law has not been applied in this way. As Baris Tansever, chairman of the Tourism, Restaurants, Club Investors and Operators group, puts it: "I don't think this will be a problem as long as you have a license to sell open bottle alcohol."

Despite suspicions that the AKP has an agenda to Islamize the country, the facts seem to prove the opposite. According to Emre Akoz, a sociologist, the trend of conservatism in Turkey loses strength as society becomes more modern and developed. "As people go along with modernization and economic and intellectual development, they become less conservative. The increase in alcohol consumption stands as proof of this," Akoz told *Asia Times Online*.

European Youths Are Starting to Drink More Like Young People in the United States

Christopher Sopher

Christopher Sopher is a journalist. In the following viewpoint, he maintains that evidence shows that the perceived difference in the youth drinking cultures in America and Europe is less than many people think. Sopher reports that studies show that European youths drink more than their US counterparts in general. There is also a generational shift: While European young people are drinking less frequently than their parents and grandparents, they are drinking more alcohol on those occasions.

As you read, consider the following questions:

1. Does the author believe that lowering the drinking age will encourage responsible drinking in American youth?

2. According to the US Department of Justice, which country—Britain or the United States—has the higher rate of binge drinking between the ages of fifteen and sixteen?

3. What is the trend of "botellón" in Spain, according to Sopher?

M any Americans idolize a culture where Europeans—accustomed to alcohol after years of experience in their teenage years—supposedly know how to avoid binge drinking,

Christopher Sopher, "How We Get Hammered: The European vs. US Drinking Age," thenextgreatgeneration.com, July 28, 2010. Reprinted by permission.

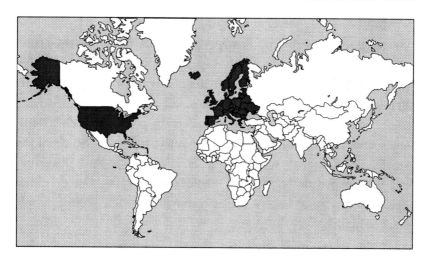

alcohol poisoning and hazy nights of bad judgment. It's a particularly popular topic of conversation among 19-year-old college students, waiting in grocery store parking lots for older friends to bring out cases of beer. "The drinking age is so stupid," they say. "If only it was like it is in Europe," suggesting with little sense of irony that, were the drinking age lower, they would both drink more moderately and enjoy the newfound freedom to buy $11 cases of Natural Light.

Looking Toward European Drinking Culture

In theory, it's a winning idea for all involved. Young people can drink earlier in their lives, which promises more of the freedom from judgment and reason teenagers desire. Parents can believe their children are getting important early experience that, as in any other sport, helps them become better players—and helps them get a head start on the 10,000 hours of practice [writer] Malcolm Gladwell says are necessary to become an expert at something. And the data shows many European and American young people are already well on their way.

But the evidence also suggests the differences between how young people drink in Europe and the United States aren't nearly as great as we imagine—and the generational changes are tremendous. By most measures, European youth actually drink more, get drunk more, and do so earlier in life than their American peers (though in certain settings, such as colleges and universities, American youth still lead the drinking world). And there's surprisingly little evidence that introducing young people to alcohol earlier or lowering the drinking age does anything except lower the age at which young people start to drink.

"The number of British, German, Scandinavian and other teenagers stumbling into hostels at 5 a.m. in London, Paris or Prague is pretty overwhelming," said one American college student traveling in Europe, who asked not to be named discussing drinking. "Lax drinking laws, a low drinking age, and a plethora of discos, bars and clubs give kids a lot of opportunities to get totally out of control."

By most measures, European youth actually drink more, get drunk more, and do so earlier in life than their American peers (though in certain settings, such as colleges and universities, American youth still lead the drinking world).

Drink Trends

Survey data and the concern of European officials support her observation. A 2008 survey found that "while young people in most European countries are drinking less frequently than their parents and grandparents, they are consuming more alcohol each time they drink," which is similar to the U.S. trend of infrequent but heavy drinking. Data from major surveys compiled by the U.S. Department of Justice found that the U.S. had lower rates of drinking and binge drinking among

The Harm Done by Binge Drinking

Alcohol is a toxic substance that can harm almost any system or organ of the body, and is related to more than 60 different disorders with short- and long-term consequences. For many conditions there is an increasing risk with increasing levels of alcohol consumption, with no evidence of a threshold effect below which alcohol can be regarded as entirely risk free. Alcohol use and a pattern of binge drinking are associated with an increased risk to the individual of negative social consequences, reduced work performance, injuries, drink-driving accidents, brain damage, alcohol dependence, suicide, stroke, irregular heart rhythms, coronary heart disease, sexually transmitted diseases, and premature death. Alcohol use and a pattern of binge drinking are associated with an increased risk to people other than the drinker (third-party harm) including negative social consequences, injuries at work, violence and crime, interpersonal violence, accidents from others' drink-driving, sexually transmitted diseases, and to the unborn child, a range of neuro-behavioural deficits running through to adolescence and with lifelong consequences.

Deutsche Hauptstelle für Suchtfragen e.V. (DHS),
"Binge Drinking and Europe," Hamm, Germany: DHS. 2008.

15–16-year-olds than every European country except Turkey (which, as a predominantly Muslim country, has strong cultural stigmas against alcohol).

"Drinking to get drunk" has become much more common in Europe over the past two decades, with several surveys reporting a growing number of teenagers and young adults who say they drink for the "buzz" or to "get [insert your favorite term for drunkenness]."

"Binge drinking culture is definitely growing in Europe, and alcoholism has always been a problem," said Charles Pellegrin, a French graduate student who has lived in several countries.

Traditionally beer-oriented countries such as the UK, Ireland, Denmark and Germany lead the statistics on youth drinking, drunkenness and alcohol-related problems—but wine countries appear to be catching up as French, Spanish and Italian young people choose beer and liquor over wine, and choose it in larger quantities.

Several Spanish and American students I interviewed discussed the trend of "botellón," (literally "big bottle") where Spanish teenagers sit outside in parks or on the street and drink together. This summer [2010] France has been overrun by the phenomenon called "apéro géant" ("giant aperitif"), where thousands of young people gather in flash mobs in French cities to party and drink very, very heavily.

The evidence suggests that the differences in drinking culture between American and European youth aren't as tremendous as we often assume.

All of this suggests that the merits of a lower drinking age and of early familiarization with alcohol might be something of a myth, too. In many European countries, the discussion about binge drinking is focused on 13-, 14- and 15-year-olds, not college students. Many European authorities are encouraging parents to take a more active role in educating their children about, and discouraging them from, drinking.

"I think that a lower drinking age just causes binge drinking a little earlier," said one American student who studied abroad in Spain.

The evidence suggests that the differences in drinking culture between American and European youth aren't as tremendous as we often assume. And in a globalized world where you can buy a Bacardi Breezer in 30 languages, that isn't surprising. The differences seem more subtle, more cultural.

"Much like in the U.S., there are parties that result in people being a little too drunk," said the American living in Switzerland. "I think that is the same across the globe, but here in Europe, alcohol is less frowned upon. But I can say for sure, when kids celebrate their sixteenth or eighteenth birthday over here, there is no focus of, 'Yes! Now we can drink!'"

Alcohol Blamed for Half of '90s Russian Deaths

Associated Press

The Associated Press (AP) is a global news network. In the following viewpoint, AP finds that the sharp escalation of alcohol abuse in Russia in the post–Soviet Union era has led to shocking health and social problems in the country, including a spike in mortality that can be directly attributed to alcohol addiction. The rise in alcohol consumption in Russia can be traced back to the collapse of the Soviet Union that produced a political instability that had a profound economic and social effect on Russian society. Many officials also factor in the key role vodka plays in Russian tradition and blame the consumption of poorly regulated industrial alcohol for the rise in alcohol-related deaths.

As you read, consider the following questions:

1. How many millions of Russian deaths does David Zaridze blame on increased alcohol consumption during the survey period?
2. According to the *Lancet* report, how many liters of pure ethanol alcohol does every Russian drink per year on average?
3. What is the average life expectancy of a Russian male born in 2006, according to the United Nations?

Associated Press, "Alcohol Blamed for Half of '90s Russian Deaths: Social and Economic Shocks of Soviet Collapse Decimate Population," MSNBC.com, June 25, 2009. Reprinted by permission.

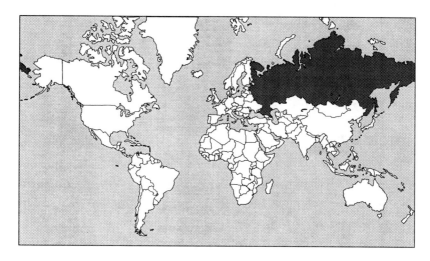

Moscow—A new study by an international team of public health researchers documents the devastating impact of alcohol abuse on Russia—showing that drinking caused more than half of deaths among Russians aged 15 to 54 in the turbulent era following the Soviet collapse.

The 52 percent figure compares to estimates that less than 4 percent of deaths worldwide are caused by alcohol abuse, according to the study by Russian, British and French researchers published in Friday's edition of the British medical journal the *Lancet.*

The Russian findings were based on a survey of almost 49,000 deaths between 1990 and 2001 among young adult and middle-aged Russians in three industrial towns in western Siberia, which had typical 1990s Russian mortality patterns.

Professor David Zaridze, head of the Russian Cancer Research Center and lead author of the study, estimated that the increase in alcohol consumption since 1987, the year when then Soviet leader Mikhail Gorbachev's restrictions on alcohol sales collapsed, cost the lives of 3 million Russians who would otherwise be alive today. "This loss is similar to that of a war," Zaridze said.

Dr. Murray Feshbach, a senior scholar at the Woodrow Wilson Center for Scholars and a leading expert on Russian public health, called the study "very impressive, very substantive" and the overall methodologically sound. He was not part of the research team.

Tragic Die-Off

The tragic die-off was largely invisible outside of Russia, but devastated Russian society—claiming the lives of millions during what should have been their most productive years. The study is part of a long-running debate among public health scientists as to the causes of an unprecedented spike in mortality among Russians in the post-Soviet era.

Some researchers have blamed the crumbling of the Soviet health care system, increased smoking, changes in diet or a loss of jobs that raised stress levels for the mysterious rise in deaths.

Many others, like Zaridze and his team, pin the blame squarely on increased drinking, which the report says roughly doubled in Russia between 1987 and 1994—from the equivalent of about 5 liters (1.3 gallons) of pure alcohol annually to about 10.5 liters (2.8 gallons).

"If you look at the dynamics of death and the dynamics of alcohol consumption in Russia, it is obvious that all these sharp increases and decreases of the mortality level are caused by increases and decreases in alcohol consumption," Zaridze said.

The scientist argued that the social and economic shocks of the late 1980s and 1990s drove people to drink.

"Alcohol consumption is always connected with poverty," he said. "It's been associated with social crisis. If we take our mortality statistics, it will be obvious that it's parallel to our social crisis, to our social instability."

Russia and some of its eastern European neighbors still have the world's highest levels of alcohol consumption, according to another study also published in the *Lancet* on Friday as part of a series on alcohol and global health.

Two other papers in the series called for stronger government policies worldwide to reduce the dangers of alcohol abuse.

Double the Global Average

Russians currently consume almost twice the global average, the equivalent of 6.2 liters (1.64 gallons) of pure ethanol alcohol per year, the global report found.

Although life expectancy here has risen slightly in recent years, Russia still has one of the lowest in Europe.

According to the most recent U.N. National Human Development Report on Russia, males born in Russia in 2006 could only expect to live to just over 60 years, while a woman born that year could expect to live on average about 73 years. By comparison, the average western European man could expect to live to be 77, about 17 years longer than his Russian counterpart.

The average western European woman could expect to live to be 82, about nine years longer than the average Russian woman.

Moderate drinking is considered healthy by many Russians, and few major events are celebrated without raising a 100-gram glass or two—or three—of vodka.

The *Lancet*'s Russian study was based on a long-term, large-scale study of drinking patterns and deaths in three industrial cities in western Siberia: Barnaul, Biysk and Omsk.

Researchers conducted tens of thousands of personal interviews and mined death records in gathering data for the report. They reported finding a strong link between heavy drink-

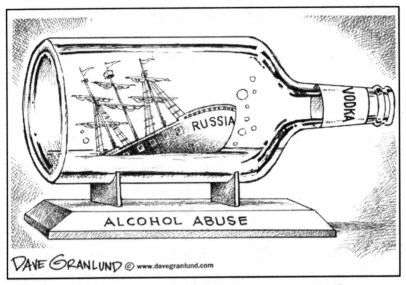

ing and causes of death associated with high alcohol abuse, including alcohol poisoning, trauma, pneumonia and liver disease.

The link between life expectancy and alcohol in Russia has long been the subject of study. Mortality rates fell sharply in Russia from late 1985 to 1987, when then Soviet leader Mikhail Gorbachev imposed strict limits on alcohol sales. During the period of political and social revolution that followed, death rates soared to levels unprecedented in modern industrialized nations.

By 2000, the report noted, the chances that a 15-year-old Russian male would die before his 35th birthday was one in ten. In Europe, the chances of a 15-year-old male dying by age 35 was one in 50.

Vodka's Integral Role

Part of the problem may be the important cultural role vodka and alcohol play in Russian society. Moderate drinking is considered healthy by many Russians, and few major events are celebrated without raising a 100-gram glass or two—or three—of vodka.

"If the soul needs it—we drink, if the soul doesn't need it—we don't drink," said Alexei Kitayev, a St. Petersburg cab driver. "Do I drink often? Beer after work to relax, vodka and beer at the weekends with my family at dinner—it's good for me and the soul is happy."

Russians generally blame alcohol deaths on the consumption of adulterated or industrial alcohol. Maxim Vdovin, an unemployed St. Petersburg resident, voiced the commonly held view here that many Russians die because the state does not control the sale of adulterated spirits.

"No one gives a damn," Vdovin said. "So many people are dying because of this raw vodka and they don't give a damn, everybody is drinking and so many people die," he said.

A previous study carried out by British and Russian researchers and published in the *Lancet* in 2007 estimated that drinking alcohol not meant for consumption like cologne and antiseptics was responsible for nearly half of all deaths among working-age Russian men.

A recent government crackdown on the sale of alcohol not intended for human consumption appears to have significantly cut those deaths, experts say.

But there is relatively little recognition here that excessive drinking of alcohol in any form, including beer and wine, can lead to serious health problems.

Periodical and Internet Sources Bibliography

The following articles have been selected to supplement the diverse views presented in this chapter.

Tania Branigan	"The Rise of Binge Drinking in China," *Guardian*, August 22, 2011.
Nicholas Köhler	"Recession? (Hic!) What Recession?," *Maclean's*, January 14, 2009.
Louisa Lim	"Widespread Alcohol Abuse Clouds Mongolia's Future," NPR.org, September 9, 2009. www.npr.org.
Denise Mann	"More Americans Drinking (Alcohol)," CNN.com, July 20, 2010. www.cnn.com.
Janet Morrissey	"In Recession, Drinking Moves from Bars to Home," *Time*, August 3, 2010.
Eric Nagourney	"Patterns: Drinking Age Affects Binging, to a Point," *New York Times*, June 29, 2009.
Cian Nihill	"Europeans 'Heaviest Drinkers in the World,'" *Irish Times*, September 13, 2011.
Julia Reed	"The Return of Legal Absinthe," The Daily Beast, March 31, 2010. www.thedailybeast.com.
David Sessions	"Does the World Have a Drinking Problem?," The Daily Beast, February 18, 2011. www.thedailybeast.com.
Michael White	"Boozing Oldies—Not the Real Issue?," *Guardian*, June 22, 2011.
World Health Organization	"Trends in Alcohol Consumption," January 14, 2011.

CHAPTER 2

Strategies to Curb Alcohol Abuse

Global Attempts to Prevent Alcohol Abuse Have Had Limited Success

World Health Organization

The World Health Organization (WHO) is the United Nations agency that focuses on international health policy. In the following viewpoint, WHO officials consider the harmful use of alcohol to be one of the main risk factors in poor global health. There are considerable challenges in formulating effective global or national programs dealing with the problem. A global strategy to support national and local efforts to curb the damage attributable to alcohol abuse is key to a more efficacious strategy.

As you read, consider the following questions:

1. According to WHO, how many people died worldwide of alcohol-related causes in 2004?
2. What does WHO say is the vision behind the global strategy to reduce alcohol abuse?
3. What three things does WHO cite as determining factors in the harmful use of alcohol and its related public health problems?

The harmful use of alcohol has a serious effect on public health and is considered to be one of the main risk factors for poor health globally. In the context of this draft strat-

World Health Organization, "2. The Global Strategy to Reduce the Harmful Use of Alcohol," *Global Strategy to Reduce the Harmful Use of Alcohol*, who.int, 2010, pp. 5–9. Reprinted by permission.

egy, the concept of the harmful use of alcohol is broad and encompasses the drinking that causes detrimental health and social consequences for the drinker, the people around the drinker and society at large, as well as the patterns of drinking that are associated with increased risk of adverse health outcomes. The harmful use of alcohol compromises both individual and social development. It can ruin the lives of individuals, devastate families, and damage the fabric of communities.

The harmful use of alcohol is a significant contributor to the global burden of disease and is listed as the third leading risk factor for premature deaths and disabilities in the world. It is estimated that 2.5 million people worldwide died of alcohol-related causes in 2004, including 320,000 young people between 15 and 29 years of age. Harmful use of alcohol was responsible for 3.8% of all deaths in the world in 2004 and 4.5% of the global burden of disease as measured in disability-adjusted life years lost, even when consideration is given to the modest protective effects, especially on coronary heart disease, of low consumption of alcohol for some people aged 40 years or older.

More Effects of Harmful Drinking

Harmful drinking is a major avoidable risk factor for neuropsychiatric disorders and other noncommunicable diseases such as cardiovascular diseases, cirrhosis of the liver and various cancers. For some diseases there is no evidence of a threshold effect in the relationship between the risk and level of alcohol consumption. The harmful use of alcohol is also associated with several infectious diseases like HIV/AIDS, tuberculosis and pneumonia. A significant proportion of the disease burden attributable to harmful drinking arises from unintentional and intentional injuries, including those due to road traffic crashes and violence, and suicides. Fatal injuries attributable to alcohol consumption tend to occur in relatively young people.

The degree of risk for harmful use of alcohol varies with age, sex and other biological characteristics of the consumer as well as with the setting and context in which the drinking takes place. Some vulnerable or at-risk groups and individuals have increased susceptibility to the toxic, psychoactive and dependence-producing properties of ethanol. At the same time low risk patterns of alcohol consumption at the individual level may not be associated with occurrence or significantly increased probability of negative health and social consequences.

A substantial scientific knowledge base exists for policy makers on the effectiveness and cost-effectiveness of strategies and interventions to prevent and reduce alcohol-related harm. Although much of the evidence comes from high-income countries, the results of meta-analyses and reviews of the available evidence provide sufficient knowledge to inform policy recommendations in terms of comparative effectiveness and cost-effectiveness of selected policy measures. With better awareness, there are increased responses at national, regional and global levels. However, these policy responses are often fragmented and do not always correspond to the magnitude of the impact on health and social development.

Unless this problem is given the attention it deserves, the spread of harmful drinking practices and norms will continue.

Challenges and Opportunities

The present commitment to reducing the harmful use of alcohol provides a great opportunity for improving health and social well-being and for reducing the existing alcohol-attributable disease burden. However, there are considerable challenges that have to be taken into account in global or national initiatives or programmes. These include the following:

(a) Increasing global action and international cooperation. The current relevant health, cultural and market trends worldwide mean that harmful use of alcohol will continue to be a global health issue. These trends should be recognized and appropriate responses implemented at all levels. In this respect, there is a need for global guidance and increased international collaboration to support and complement regional and national actions.

(b) Ensuring intersectoral action. The diversity of alcohol-related problems and measures necessary to reduce alcohol-related harm points to the need for comprehensive action across numerous sectors. Policies to reduce the harmful use of alcohol must reach beyond the health sector, and appropriately engage such sectors as development, transport, justice, social welfare, fiscal policy, trade, agriculture, consumer policy, education and employment, as well as civil society and economic operators.

(c) According appropriate attention. Preventing and reducing harmful use of alcohol is often given a low priority among decision makers despite compelling evidence of its serious public health effects. In addition, there is a clear discrepancy between the increasing availability and affordability of alcohol beverages in many developing and low- and middle-income countries and those countries' capability and capacity to meet the additional public health burden that follows. Unless this problem is given the attention it deserves, the spread of harmful drinking practices and norms will continue.

(d) Balancing different interests. Production, distribution, marketing and sales of alcohol create employment and generate considerable income for economic operators and tax revenue for governments at different levels. Public health measures to reduce harmful use of alcohol are sometimes judged to be in conflict with other goals like free markets and consumer choice and can be seen as harming economic interests and reducing government revenues. Policy makers face the challenge of giving an appropriate priority to the promotion and protection of population health while taking into account other goals, obligations, including international legal obligations, and interests. It should be noted in this respect that international trade agreements generally recognize the right of countries to take measures to protect human health, provided that these are not applied in a manner which would constitute a means of unjustifiable or arbitrary discrimination or disguised restrictions to trade. In this regard, national, regional and international efforts should take into account the impact of harmful use of alcohol.

(e) Focusing on equity. Population-wide rates of drinking of alcoholic beverages are markedly lower in poorer societies than in wealthier ones. However, for a given amount of consumption, poorer populations may experience disproportionately higher levels of alcohol-attributable harm. There is a great need to develop and implement effective policies and programmes that reduce such social disparities both inside a country and between countries. Such policies are also needed in order to generate and disseminate new knowledge about the complex relationship between harmful consumption of alcohol and social and health inequity, particularly among indigenous populations, minority or marginalized groups and in developing countries.

(f) Considering the "context" in recommending actions. Much of the published evidence of effectiveness of alcohol-related policy interventions comes from high-income countries, and concerns have been expressed that their effectiveness depends on context and may not be transferrable to other settings. However, many interventions to reduce harmful use of alcohol have been implemented in a wide variety of cultures and settings, and their results are often consistent and in line with the underpinning theories and evidence base accumulated in other similar public health areas. The focus for those developing and implementing policies should be on appropriate tailoring of effective interventions to accommodate local contexts and on appropriate monitoring and evaluation to provide feedback for further action.

(g) Strengthening information. Systems for collecting, analysing and disseminating data on alcohol consumption, alcohol-related harm and policy responses have been developed by member states [of the United Nations], the WHO [World Health Organization] secretariat, and some other stakeholders. There are still substantial gaps in knowledge and it is important to sharpen the focus on information and knowledge production and dissemination for further developments in this area, especially in developing and low- and middle-income countries. The WHO Global Information System on Alcohol and Health and integrated regional information systems provide the means to monitor better progress made in reducing harmful use of alcohol at the global and regional levels.

Aims and Objectives

National and local efforts can produce better results when they are supported by regional and global action within agreed policy frames. Thus the purpose of the global strategy is to support and complement public health policies in member states.

The vision behind the global strategy is improved health and social outcomes for individuals, families and communities, with considerably reduced morbidity and mortality due

Ways to Reduce the Burden from Harmful Use of Alcohol

The health, safety and socioeconomic problems attributable to alcohol can be effectively reduced and require actions on the levels, patterns and contexts of alcohol consumption and the wider social determinants of health.

Countries have a primary responsibility for formulating, implementing, monitoring and evaluating public policies to reduce the harmful use of alcohol. A substantial scientific knowledge base exists for policy makers on the effectiveness and cost-effectiveness of the following strategies:

- regulating the marketing of alcoholic beverages, (in particular to younger people);

- regulating and restricting availability of alcohol;

- enacting appropriate drink-driving policies;

- reducing demand through taxation and pricing mechanisms;

- raising awareness and support for policies;

- providing accessible and affordable treatment for people with alcohol-use disorders; and

- implementing screening programmes and brief interventions for hazardous and harmful use of alcohol.

World Health Organization, "Alcohol,"
Fact Sheet #349, February 2011. www.who.int.

to harmful use of alcohol and their ensuing social consequences. It is envisaged that the global strategy will promote and support local, regional and global actions to prevent and reduce the harmful use of alcohol.

The global strategy aims to give guidance for action at all levels; to set priority areas for global action; and to recommend a portfolio of policy options and measures that could be considered for implementation and adjusted as appropriate at the national level, taking into account national circumstances, such as religious and cultural contexts, national public health priorities, as well as resources, capacities and capabilities.

The strategy has five objectives:

(a) raised global awareness of the magnitude and nature of the health, social and economic problems caused by harmful use of alcohol, and increased commitment by governments to act to address the harmful use of alcohol;

(b) strengthened knowledge base on the magnitude and determinants of alcohol-related harm and on effective interventions to reduce and prevent such harm;

(c) increased technical support to, and enhanced capacity of, member states for preventing the harmful use of alcohol and managing alcohol-use disorders and associated health conditions;

(d) strengthened partnerships and better coordination among stakeholders and increased mobilization of resources required for appropriate and concerted action to prevent the harmful use of alcohol;

(e) improved systems for monitoring and surveillance at different levels, and more effective dissemination and application of information for advocacy, policy development and evaluation purposes.

The harmful use of alcohol and its related public health problems are influenced by the general level of alcohol consumption in a population, drinking patterns and local contexts. Achieving the five objectives will require global, regional and national actions on the levels, patterns and contexts of alcohol consumption and the wider social determinants of health. Special attention needs to be given to reducing harm to people other than the drinker and to populations that are at particular risk from harmful use of alcohol, such as children, adolescents, women of child-bearing age, pregnant and breastfeeding women, indigenous peoples and other minority groups or groups with low socioeconomic status.

Guiding Principles

The protection of the health of the population by preventing and reducing the harmful use of alcohol is a public health priority. The following principles will guide the development and implementation of policies at all levels; they reflect the multi-faceted determinants of alcohol-related harm and the concerted multi-sectoral actions required to implement effective interventions.

(a) Public policies and interventions to prevent and reduce alcohol-related harm should be guided and formulated by public health interests and based on clear public health goals and the best available evidence.

(b) Policies should be equitable and sensitive to national, religious and cultural contexts.

(c) All involved parties have the responsibility to act in ways that do not undermine the implementation of public policies and interventions to prevent and reduce harmful use of alcohol.

(d) Public health should be given proper deference in relation to competing interests, and approaches that support that direction should be promoted.

(e) Protection of populations at high risk of alcohol-attributable harm and those exposed to the effects of harmful drinking by others should be an integral part of policies addressing the harmful use of alcohol.

(f) Individuals and families affected by the harmful use of alcohol should have access to affordable and effective prevention and care services.

(g) Children, teenagers and adults who choose not to drink alcohol beverages have the right to be supported in their non-drinking behaviour and protected from pressures to drink.

(h) Public policies and interventions to prevent and reduce alcohol-related harm should encompass all alcoholic beverages and surrogate alcohol.

The United States Should Lower Its Drinking Age

John M. McCardell Jr.

John M. McCardell Jr. is the vice chancellor of the University of the South. In the following viewpoint, he argues that the prevailing belief that the act of raising the American drinking age to twenty-one in 1984 was a success is a myth. In fact, he points out, binge drinking on college campuses is on the rise despite attempts to clamp down on underage drinking. McCardell suggests that there should be a meaningful debate on lowering the US drinking age and that serious attempts to better educate young people on the harmful effects of binge drinking and the importance of observing all drinking laws should be implemented.

As you read, consider the following questions:

1. According to a study published in the *Journal of the American Academy of Child and Adolescent Psychiatry*, to what extent has binge drinking by college women escalated since 1979?

2. What will any state that lowers its drinking age forfeit, according to a provision of the 1984 drinking age law?

3. How many lives of Americans under the age of twenty-one does the author cite as being lost every year to alcohol-related causes?

John M. McCardell Jr., "Drinking Age of 21 Doesn't Work," CNN.com, September 16, 2009. Reprinted by permission.

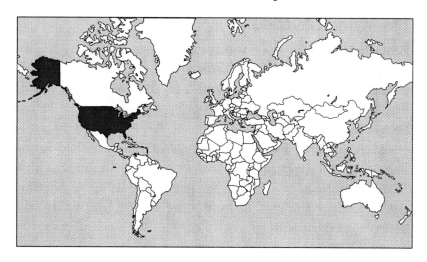

One year ago [2008], a group of college and university presidents and chancellors, eventually totaling 135, issued a statement that garnered national attention.

The Amethyst Initiative

The "Amethyst Initiative" put a debate proposition before the public—"Resolved: That the 21-year-old drinking age is not working." It offered, in much the way a grand jury performs its duties, sufficient evidence for putting the proposition to the test. It invited informed and dispassionate public debate and committed the signatory institutions to encouraging that debate. And it called on elected officials not to continue assuming that, after 25 years, the status quo could not be challenged, even improved.

One year later, the drinking age debate continues, and new research reinforces the presidential impulse. Just this summer a study published in the *Journal of the American Academy of Child and Adolescent Psychiatry* revealed that, among college-age males, binge drinking is unchanged from its levels of 1979; that among non-college women it has increased by 20 percent; and that among college women it has increased by 40 percent.

The Myth of Success

Remarkably, the counterintuitive conclusion drawn by the investigators, and accepted uncritically by the media, including editorials in the *New York Times* and the *Washington Post* is that the study proves that raising the drinking age to 21 has been a success.

More recently, a study of binge drinking published in the *Journal of the American Medical Association* announced that "despite efforts at prevention, the prevalence of binge drinking among college students is continuing to rise, and so are the harms associated with it."

In the face of mounting evidence that those young adults age 18 to 20 toward whom the drinking age law has been directed are routinely—indeed in life- and health-threatening ways—violating it, there remains a belief in the land that a minimum drinking age of 21 has been a "success."

Worse still, a related study has shown that habits formed at 18 die hard: "For each year studied, a greater percentage of 21- to 24-year-olds [those who were of course once 18, 19 and 20] engaged in binge drinking and driving under the influence of alcohol."

Yet, in the face of mounting evidence that those young adults age 18 to 20 toward whom the drinking age law has been directed are routinely—indeed in life- and health-threatening ways—violating it, there remains a belief in the land that a minimum drinking age of 21 has been a "success." And elected officials are periodically reminded of a provision in the 1984 law that continues to stifle any serious public debate in our country's state legislative chambers: Any state that sets its drinking age lower than 21 forfeits 10 percent of its annual federal highway appropriation.

But it's not 1984 anymore.

The Old Problem

This statement may seem obvious, but not necessarily. In 1984 Congress passed and the president signed the National Minimum Drinking Age Act. The act, which raised the drinking age to 21 under threat of highway fund withholding, sought to address the problem of drunken driving fatalities. And indeed, that problem was serious.

States that lowered their ages during the 1970s and did nothing else to prepare young adults to make responsible decisions about alcohol witnessed an alarming increase in alcohol-related traffic fatalities. It was as though the driving age was lowered but no driver's education was provided. The results were predictable.

Now, 25 years later, we are in a much different, and better, place. Thanks to the effective public advocacy of organizations like Mothers Against Drunk Driving, we are far more aware of the risks of drinking and driving. Automobiles are much safer.

Seat belts and airbags are mandatory. The "designated driver" is now a part of our vocabulary. And more and more states are mandating ignition interlocks for first-time DUI [driving under the influence] offenders, perhaps the most effective way to get drunken drivers off the road.

And the statistics are encouraging. Alcohol-related fatalities have declined over the last 25 years. Better still, they have declined in all age groups, though the greatest number of deaths occurs at age 21, followed by 22 and 23. We are well on the way to solving a problem that vexed us 25 years ago.

The New Problem

The problem today is different. The problem today is reckless, goal-oriented alcohol consumption that all too often takes place in clandestine locations, where enforcement has proven frustratingly difficult. Alcohol consumption among young adults is not taking place in public places or public view or in

US Binge Drinking

- Approximately 92% of U.S. adults who drink excessively report binge drinking in the past 30 days.

- Although college students commonly binge drink, 70% of binge drinking episodes involve adults age 26 years and older.

- The prevalence of binge drinking among men is higher than the prevalence among women.

- Binge drinkers are 14 times more likely to report alcohol-impaired driving than non-binge drinkers.

- About 90% of the alcohol consumed by youth under the age of 21 in the United States is in the form of binge drinks.

- About 75% of the alcohol consumed by adults in the United States is in the form of binge drinks.

- The proportion of current drinkers that binge is highest in the 18- to 20-year-old group (51%).

Centers for Disease Control and Prevention,
"Binge Drinking," 2011. www.cdc.gov.

the presence of other adults who might help model responsible behavior. But we know it is taking place.

If not in public, then where? The college presidents who signed the Amethyst Initiative know where. It happens in "pre-gaming" sessions in locked dorm rooms where students take multiple shots of hard alcohol in rapid succession, before going to a social event where alcohol is not served. It happens in off-campus apartments beyond college boundaries and thus beyond the presidents' authority; and it happens in remote fields to which young adults must drive.

And the Amethyst presidents know the deadly result: Of the 5,000 lives lost to alcohol each year by those under 21, more than 60 percent are lost OFF the roadways, according to the National Institute on Alcohol Abuse and Alcoholism.

The principal problem of 2009 is not drunken driving. The principal problem of 2009 is clandestine binge drinking.

Addressing Binge Drinking

That is why the Amethyst presidents believe a public debate is so urgent. The law does not say drink responsibly or drink in moderation. It says don't drink. To those affected by it, those who in the eyes of the law are, in every other respect legal adults, it is Prohibition. And it is incomprehensible.

The principal impediment to public debate is the 10 percent highway penalty. That penalty should be waived for those states that choose to try something different, which may turn out to be something better. But merely adjusting the age—up or down—is not really the way to make a change.

We should prepare young adults to make responsible decisions about alcohol in the same way we prepare them to operate a motor vehicle: by first educating and then licensing, and permitting them to exercise the full privileges of adulthood so long as they demonstrate their ability to observe the law.

Licensing would work like driver's education—it would involve a permit, perhaps graduated, allowing the holder the privilege of purchasing, possessing and consuming alcohol, as each state determined, so long as the holder had passed an alcohol education course and observed the alcohol laws of the issuing state.

An Outdated and Ineffective Law

Most of the rest of the world has come out in a different place on the drinking age. The United States is one of only four countries—the others are Indonesia, Mongolia and Palau—

with an age as high as 21. All others either have no minimum age or have a lower age, generally 18, with some at 16.

Young adults know that. And, in their heart of hearts, they also know that a law perceived as unjust, a law routinely violated, can over time breed disrespect for law in general.

We can either try to change the reality—which has been our principal focus since 1984, by imposing Prohibition on young adults 18 to 20—or we can create the safest possible environment for the reality.

Slowly but surely we may be seeing a change in attitude. This summer, Dr. Morris Chafetz, a distinguished psychiatrist, a member of the presidential commission that recommended raising the drinking age, and the founder of the National Institute on Alcohol Abuse and Alcoholism, admitted that supporting the higher drinking age is "the most regrettable decision of my entire professional career." This remarkable statement did not receive the attention it merited.

Alcohol is a reality in the lives of young adults. We can either try to change the reality—which has been our principal focus since 1984, by imposing Prohibition on young adults 18 to 20—or we can create the safest possible environment for the reality.

A drinking age minimum of 21 has not changed the reality. It's time to try something different.

It's not 1984 anymore.

First Nations Communities in Canada Are Considering Alcohol Bans

Christine Sismondo and Simon Beggs

Christine Sismondo is an author and educator, and Simon Beggs is a researcher and educator. In the following viewpoint, they discuss the efficacy of self-imposed alcohol bans put in place by a number of First Nations communities in Canada. Sismondo and Beggs dispute the widespread prevalence of the firewater myth, which posits that First Nations peoples are more physically disposed toward alcohol, instead arguing that high rates of alcoholism in native communities are based on the effects of colonialism and its social, political, economic, and psychological effects.

As you read, consider the following questions:

1. When was the firewater myth forged, according to Sismondo and Beggs?
2. How many First Nations communities have put alcohol bans in place?
3. What initiatives do the authors say native communities are investing in now that the crime rate has gone down?

In 1670, sometime after English settler Daniel Denton encountered aboriginals on Long Island, he wrote, "They are great lovers of strong drink, yet do not care for drinking, un-

Christine Sismondo and Simon Beggs, "Firewater," *The Walrus*, July–August 2010. Reprinted by permission.

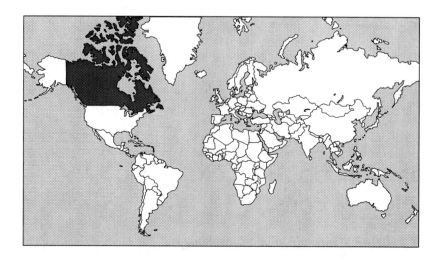

less they have enough to make themselves drunk." With this and other colonial tracts, an enduring and pejorative myth was forged: "Indians" can't handle their booze. And the "firewater myth," as it would later be called, would in turn be used to bolster a long history of government interference in native populations' access to alcohol. Just twenty-five years ago [1985], the Indian Act was finally overhauled, giving First Nations complete authority to deal with their own affairs, including those related to alcohol.

Communities Deal with the Problem of Alcohol

Meanwhile, as soon as native communities were allowed any alcoholic self-determination, starting in the '50s, many chose local prohibition. Today over 100 of some 600 band councils enforce self-imposed bans. The obvious reason is that drinking within aboriginal communities continues to be a problem. Statistics are hard to come by, but we do know that there are many more incidences of fetal alcohol syndrome on reserves than in the general population, and the majority of fatal fire and vehicular accidents on reserves turn out to be alcohol related. In Natuashish, Labrador, where residents voted to extend a two-year-old ban this past March [2010], there's no such thing as social drinking, according to former chief Katie Rich. "People drink to get drunk, and it's always been that way," she says. "The alcohol will come in, and you drink it till it's all gone and you're drunk."

In other words, binge drinking isn't unique to aboriginals (as the term "firewater myth" implies); it's a behaviour adopted by individuals to cope with the hopelessness of life on some reserves.

The Firewater Myth

Sound familiar? If anything, the firewater myth has picked up steam since early genetic studies posited that aboriginals are predisposed to enzyme variants that slow the metabolism of alcohol—and increase the rate of intoxication. Never mind that extensive research conducted over the past fifteen years hasn't found these variants in native populations (only in east Asian and African ones, and even then they seem to offer these populations some protection against alcoholism, since the hangovers are so bad). These findings are often overlooked, perhaps because the firewater myth provides a handy label for what is actually a much more difficult problem to solve.

"Most populations dissembled by colonialism experience drug and alcohol problems," says Dr. Richard Thatcher, a sociologist who has been studying problem drinking in First Nations communities for over twenty years. "And it takes many generations to resolve them." In other words, binge drinking isn't unique to aboriginals (as the term "firewater myth" implies); it's a behaviour adopted by individuals to cope with the hopelessness of life on some reserves. Thatcher understands the push for dry communities, but suggests it won't accomplish anything unless it is accompanied by initiatives that offer people incentives to plan for the long term.

The Ban's Limitations

Some in the community go further, arguing that, in the absence of such strategies, bans just drive problem drinking underground. Simeon Tshakapesh, Natuashish's new chief, says he reopened the debate about the alcohol ban in response to reports of rampant smuggling. Booze was still coming in, and commanding $350 per bottle. "A few people were afraid to come home if they'd been drinking out of town, and had to sleep outside on the Ski-Doos," he adds. It only underscores the problem that Tshakapesh has been charged with intoxication. (He has pleaded not guilty.)

"We never expected to wipe out alcohol altogether," Katie Rich says when asked about the ban's limitations. "We just wanted to get rid of the large quantities." She explains that the community was in a state of constant crisis prior to the ban; alcohol was the driving force behind a never-ending cycle of suicide, domestic violence, and petty theft. Now that crime has decreased, it's possible for the community to redirect its resources toward initiatives like the Journey, a recovery program that doesn't treat problem drinking as a genetic destiny.

Above all, Rich says, the ban reflects the community's commitment to change. It's a sign of the hopefulness that could ultimately serve as its own solution.

Scotland Must Take Drastic Action to Address Its Alcohol Culture

Pete Martin

Pete Martin is a columnist for the Scotsman. *In the following viewpoint, he describes a recent train ride during which he had to deal with a group of drunken louts—an experience he deems common in Scotland. Martin suggests that to change the drinking culture in Scotland would require decisive and effective policies, such as banning alcohol on public transportation and outlawing the sale of strong alcohol in big supermarkets.*

As you read, consider the following questions:

1. What does the author suggest as the new VisitScotland motto?
2. What is the first thing Martin lists as wrong with Scotland?
3. How would higher alcohol prices affect Scottish pubs, according to Martin?

It was a journey of two halves and the contrast couldn't have been more startling. I was on the London-Glasgow train on a Sunday afternoon. Having stood on my headphones, I couldn't listen to music or watch a movie—so the other passengers passed for entertainment.

Pete Martin, "Time for a Sober Look at Drunken Scotland," Scotsman.com, April 22, 2011. Reprinted by permission.

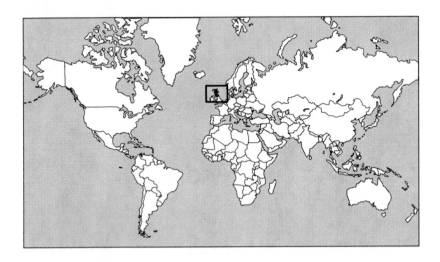

On the first half of the journey, a small child and her mother cheered me up. Seated at the coveted tables, mum had come prepared with books and colouring pens. They conversed and cuddled all the way through middle England. I assume they had a bicycle waiting at York station. For when they disembarked, in a funny touching metaphor of motherly care, the mum put a bright pink helmet on her child and the little girl proudly, happily marched off the train.

Their place was taken by eight drunk, foul-mouthed men from Motherwell. Big baldy nappers, massive beer bellies, tattoos, they brought a carry-out on to the train for a carry-on.

Drunken Conversation

It's hard to describe the strange foghorn quality of their "conversation", carried on at ear-splitting volume. You know the barking sound that followed Iain Gray into Subway the other week—as if one of [cartoon character] Marge Simpson's sisters had grown up on Clydebank and Buckfast?[1] Well, imagine that, from obese louts who think the whole world is deaf.

---

1. Demonstrators protesting funding cuts supported by Labour leader Iain Gray followed him into a Subway sandwich shop.

Only one of them had brought a newspaper and they were, literally, talking crap. They didn't mention movies or music or all the books they weren't reading. Or news or politics. Incredibly, they didn't even discuss football. Instead, they shouted about s***ing their pants and skid-marks, about getting mad-drunk and mad-drunker, about battered food and battering people.

While VisitScotland spends public millions selling the Scottish experience as "Feel it, Live it, Visit", our bold ambassadors were teaching a trainload of our neighbours to "Fear it, loathe it and get as far away from it as you can".

The drunkest of the party had obviously finished his carry-out before getting on the train. He had a walleyed glare that reminded me of American storyteller Garrison Keillor's advice for moose-rutting season: Do not make eye contact. Passing through the carriage with refreshments, the beautiful young trolley dolly handled him like a true pro, though.

"Cunnuhuvvuhbee-urrr" he slurred. She didn't understand, and didn't even pause in pulling her trolley.

"Cunnuhuvvuhbee-urrr" he said again.

"No, I think you've had enough," she smiled and glided out of the carriage, the [actress and princess] Grace Kelly of the eastern line.

A National Embarrassment

Our heroes seemed dimly aware that they were making asses of themselves and their nation. From time to time, the loudest of them would yell: "Stop swearing!" Then they'd go back to shouting about all the hilarious times they'd had together being antisocial. Like some absurd self-referential Kafkaesque nightmare, their camaraderie revolved around drinking and shouting about making a nuisance of themselves while drinking and shouting and making a nuisance of themselves. . . . If they were 17 you might understand. These guys were in their mid-40s. How did they live so long and stay so dumb?

Their best bit of banter happened when a woman with a dog went by and one of them called out "Is that dog a cat?" Obviously an in-joke, the surreal comedy was undercut when they all began to repeat the line, and then did it all over again when she returned to her seat.

At Durham, they performed the name of the city in the style of the Pink Panther theme. Funny the first time, by the 20th chorus I could take no more and switched to the eerily silent, weirdly normal next cabin.

Alcohol-related deaths and disease are rising in Scotland.

Outlining Scotland's Problems

And there you have it. In a nutshell: "What's wrong with this country."

Point 1: Education. It's a huge issue in every sense. But, suffice to say, the answer to these guys' problems wasn't two years less schooling.

Point 2: Alcohol. Whoever wins the forthcoming election, our drinking culture falls under the category of "something must be done". Alcohol-related deaths and disease are rising in Scotland. But, of course, that's only part of a picture that impacts social justice as well as criminal justice; life chances as well as welfare costs.

What Kind of Interventions Work?

Professor Sally MacIntyre of the Medical Research Council has written sensitively on the subject of health and inequality and, crucially, what kind of interventions really work. Human behaviour is complex and, certainly, a range of different measures need to be applied to effect change in a politically acceptable way. But, without wishing to caricature Prof MacIntyre's work, it's hard to avoid the interpretation that consultation is useless.

It seems high-handed, almost draconian regulatory interventions, applied fast and hard, work best. Why? Is it because a typically namby-pamby, widely consultative process simply serves to muddy the waters, delaying and diluting effective action as freely as I mix metaphors?

Alcohol Pricing

The argument on alcohol pricing is a case in point. The medical profession is bamboozled by why minimum pricing can't be introduced when it seems the big booze brands and retailers largely support it.

But this simplistic concept masks a complicated commercial reality. Minimum pricing would help the power brands fight off smaller brands that often compete by selling cheaper. Indeed, the top brands would prefer if the big retailers weren't allowed to degrade their image by using them as loss leaders.

Higher prices also create extra profit—though with the negotiating tactics of the supermarkets, it's debatable how this would be split between the retailers and the drinks manufacturers. Plus extra profits attract extra marketing. . . .

What we drink is driven by self-presentation. How much we drink and how we act under the influence is motivated by how we feel.

And then there's the state of our pubs. Higher prices would hurt licensees and could hasten the demise of community bars—when many feel it's cheap off-sales that are behind many problems.

Drink is relatively cheap because we're richer. But current prices have outstripped inflation and we've kept drinking. So culture remains the real issue, not price.

What we drink is driven by self-presentation. How much we drink and how we act under the influence is motivated by how we feel. Let me give you an example.

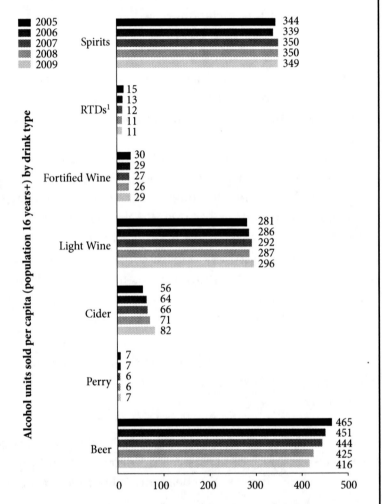

Units of Alcohol Sold Per Capita (Aged 16+) in Scotland, 2005–2009

Legend:
- 2005
- 2006
- 2007
- 2008
- 2009

Spirits
- 344
- 339
- 350
- 350
- 349

RTDs[1]
- 15
- 13
- 12
- 11
- 11

Fortified Wine
- 30
- 29
- 27
- 26
- 29

Light Wine
- 281
- 286
- 292
- 287
- 296

Cider
- 56
- 64
- 66
- 71
- 82

Perry
- 7
- 7
- 6
- 6
- 7

Beer
- 465
- 451
- 444
- 425
- 416

Y-axis: Alcohol units sold per capita (population 16 years+) by drink type

X-axis: 0, 100, 200, 300, 400, 500

1 Ready-to-drink alcoholic beverages are defined as 'pre-mixed alcoholic beverages, typically based on vodka with a flavoured mixer to create a 'long' drink'.

TAKEN FROM: NHS Health Scotland, *Alcohol Statistics Scotland 2011*. Edinburgh: NHS National Services Scotland, 2011.

The Case of the Dodgy Pub

A few years ago, some friends of mine took over a dodgy pub. They had no experience in the trade, and the local police kindly pointed out the pub's "previous"—a list of brawls, knifings and general mayhem as long as the arm of the law.

Undeterred, my friends took over the bar and, hoping to bring in a better clientele, they set about getting rid of the trouble makers.

Do you think they put the prices up? Nope. They quickly deduced what the ne'er-do-wells liked to drink—seemingly Scotland's favourite "cooking lager", a dark rum from Dundee and, for the ladies, a coconut-flavoured concoction. They simply substituted those drinks with different (but no lesser) brands at the same price. The old regulars drifted away, creating the opportunity to build a successful business in a new, more civilised bar.

Changing the Drinking Culture

So, here are two suggestions for changing the drinking culture in Scotland in a draconian way:

Firstly, no booze on public transport. Not as a carry-on, nor as off-sales from the train shop or airplane trolley. Second, and I can guarantee that the big retailers won't like this, no supermarket sales of anything stronger than mid-strength beer, say 3.5 per cent.

If that sounds crazy to you, consider the ultimate party town, New York. There, you can only buy strong drink from good old-fashioned licensed premises—a bar or an independent specialist shop.

The potential benefits are obvious.

Firstly, alcohol becomes a considered purchase and people tend to drink more considerately.

Secondly, it could encourage a new market for mid-to-low strength beers (and long drinks) where Scottish producers could excel.

Thirdly, smaller scale distribution would mean prices would inevitably be higher.

But it would redress the power balance in the booze market and also open up opportunities for local bars and off-licenses, around which other local shops might develop.

So, whoever wins the election, let's get down to the hypermarket and celebrate with alcohol that costs less than water while we still can. Because folks, every party knows: The party is over.

Germany Turns to Drinking Rooms to Address Public Drunkenness

Eric Kelsey

Eric Kelsey is a journalist and contributor to Der Spiegel. *In the following viewpoint, he reports that there is a growing movement to ban public drinking in Germany that involves changing laws regulating police authority. Regions that have been able to impose bans on public drinking have seen a significant drop in public drunkenness and crime. In Kiel, authorities have had success with a drinking room, which allows drinkers to bring their own beer or wine and congregate inside instead of loitering in public places such as town squares or parks. Other cities are interested in emulating the concept.*

As you read, consider the following questions:

1. According to law enforcement official Nils Schmid, a public drinking ban led to a crime drop of what percentage in the town of Freiburg?
2. How much did crime drop on the Metronom train after an alcohol ban, according to the author?
3. What does the author list as the unintended consequences of a public drinking ban in Berlin's Mitte district in 2009?

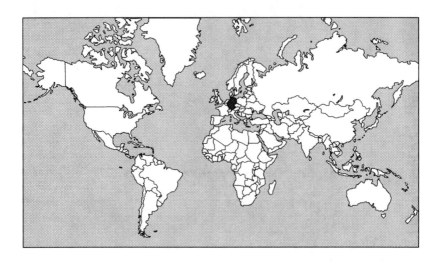

Grizzled characters clutching bottles on train station benches; groups of guzzling youth on city squares; loose empties rattling around subways: Signs of Germany's liberal public drinking laws are everywhere. Indeed, for many visitors to the country, sipping a beer while walking down the street is almost as exhilarating as a high-speed drive down the autobahn.

Increasingly, though, municipalities are tiring of public drinking—and the inevitable public drunkenness that results. Numerous movements are afoot to ban the practice. From the country's northeast to the southwest, politicians of all stripes are exploring ways to put the cap back on the bottle.

"We have a problem with alcohol consumption in public places and with people who drink too much and cause disturbances," Reinhold Gall, a state parliamentarian in Baden-Württemberg for the Social Democrats (SPD), told *Spiegel Online*. "Also, there have been complaints from store owners that nearby drinking and drunkenness chase away customers."

But simply banning public drinking is not quite as easy as it may sound. Municipalities in much of Germany do not have the authority to simply pass a general ban on alcohol in public. In Baden-Württemberg, as elsewhere, the state would have to change laws regulating police authority first—a process which is under way in the southwestern German state.

Short Lived

"We want to give cities and towns the ability to ban alcohol in certain public places," Peter Hauk, the floor leader for the Christian Democrats in Baden-Württemberg's state parliament, told *Spiegel Online*. Hauk's CDU [Christian Democratic Union] governs the state in a coalition with the pro-business Free Democrats (FDP), which has yet to grant its approval to the plan.

From the country's northeast to the southwest, politicians of all stripes are exploring ways to put the cap back on the bottle.

For many in the state, the rationale behind banning alcohol in public places isn't just a nuisance issue. Nils Schmid, head of the SPD in the state, has framed it as a crime prevention strategy. In his springtime campaign for a ban, Schmid emphasized that violent crime fell by 16 percent during a ban in the university town of Freiburg.

That regulation, however, was short lived. It was thrown out by a regional court in July 2009, just 18 months after it was introduced. The reason? The ban was too broad, the court found. A ban in the town of Magdeburg was lifted for a similar reason.

Schmid, though, thinks cities need to be able to ban alcohol in certain areas to prevent violence. "A ban on alcohol is not a party-killer," Schmid told critics at the time.

What's Wrong with an After-Work Beer?

That's where some disagree. A debate broke out this spring in Hamburg over an attempt to ban alcohol on public transit within the city after alcohol was thought to have played a part in the murder of a 19-year-old on a commuter train platform.

A Win-Win Situation at the Sofa

So far the Kiel experiment has worked. Unemployed alcoholics who are known to the authorities, and who had previously come into conflict with citizens during their drinking binges in the city's downtown area, have gradually moved to the more welcoming Sofa.

Guido Kleinhubbert,
"Germany's First Drinking Room for Alcoholics,"
Der Spiegel, April 21, 2010.

Proponents of a ban in Hamburg pointed to Metronom, a private regional train company that serves the city, which saw crime drop 70 percent shortly after it banned alcohol on its trains in November 2009.

But critics in Hamburg argue that such a ban unfairly targets law-abiding citizens. "Why should we prevent someone who drinks quietly and peacefully from having his after-work beer? Or a group of friends from opening a little champagne as they head out on the town?" Peter Kellermann, the head of the Hamburg transit authority, said during the debate in May.

Kellermann contended that it would be unfeasible to enforce an alcohol ban on its trains. There are too many passengers, too many trains and too few security personnel, he said. As a compromise, the transit authority agreed to assess a €15 [euro] fine to any misconduct under the influence of alcohol, launching an ad campaign to discourage irresponsible drinking and training security personnel to deal with drunkards.

Public Ban Not a Suitable Solution

Such reluctance to ban public drinking is hardly surprising in Germany. As in other countries in Europe, many see the ability to sip a beer while walking down the street almost as a natural-born right. But alcohol abuse—particularly youth binge drinking—has been a topic of national debate in recent years, as has public drunkenness.

"A strategy of prevention would be much more effective as a solution than a ban on alcohol in public," Tilo Berner, spokesman for the Green Party in Baden-Württemberg, told *Spiegel Online*. "Such a law would be problematic from a civil rights perspective. It says that everyone who drinks is a problem."

It is partially out of such concerns that many municipalities have begun exploring other ways to get public drinking—in particular public drunkenness—under control. Many of those efforts have been modeled after a program in the northern German city of Kiel.

In 2003, the city established a drinking room for alcoholics. Known as the Sofa, it is a place where drinkers can bring their own beer or wine—hard liquor is not allowed—instead of besieging public spaces as before.

"Win-Win Situation"

Several cities have recently shown an interest in emulating the concept, including Berlin, Hamburg, Dortmund and even Freiburg. It's also "much easier to reach" alcoholics, says Christoph Schneider of the Kiel housing office. After seven years of operation, the Sofa has been called a "win-win situation" by the city.

Hamburg's Mitte district hopes to secure funding for its own drinking room this fall. "No other proposal seems to have worked," Kerstin Gröhn, an SPD representative for the district, told *Spiegel Online*. "We don't view a public ban as a suitable solution."

Still, alcohol bans are proving popular this year [2010] with several local governments set to consider the issue this fall. Like Baden-Württemberg, the eastern German state of

Saxony-Anhalt seeks to pass a law this year which would make it legal for municipalities in the state to push through public drinking bans.

Elsewhere in Germany, Aachen on the Belgium border, Potsdam outside of Berlin and Aulendorf, a spa town of about 10,000 residents near Switzerland, are all pushing for bans or have already put them in place.

Drinkers Go Elsewhere

Still, public bans don't always lead to happier citizens. Berlin's Mitte district banned alcohol in parks in 2009 to the relief of many residents. But the park ordinance had undesired consequences. The large drinking scene around Leopoldplatz north of the city center merely moved into the side streets around the park, increasing the imposition on local residents. The district lifted the ban earlier this year.

"The strategy of repression has been attempted for many years," Franz Schulz, the mayor of Berlin's Kreuzberg district, told *Spiegel Online*. "Drinkers just move to other areas."

Public bans don't always lead to happier citizens.

Schulz's district opened its own isolated public area for drinkers last year, following complaints from residents. This fall, Schulz hopes to secure between €130,000 and €150,000 for a second drinking area that will come complete with a toilet and a stand where alcoholics and addicts can receive counselling.

For Schulz, an alcohol ban is off the table. "Prohibition is not a lasting and peaceful solution," he says. "It requires too many police officers. Anyway, drinkers are citizens too, with the same rights we all have."

Russia's Attempts to Curb Vodka Consumption Do Not Address the Root of the Problem

Kate Transchel

Kate Transchel is an author and professor of Russian and Eastern European history at California State University. In the following viewpoint, she maintains that a new law in Russia setting a minimum price for vodka—in effect, doubling the price— will lead to cheap liquor and moonshine flooding the market. Transchel argues the law, which aims at combating alcohol abuse, will fail like numerous earlier attempts by Russian leaders because it ignores the root social and economic causes of the high alcoholism rate in Russia.

As you read, consider the following questions:

1. According to a 1991 study, where do Russians drink alcohol more: home, bars, or work?
2. When does the author say the first all-out effort to combat drinking in Russia occurred?
3. What happened when Mikhail Gorbachev attempted to combat alcoholism in the 1980s, according to Transchel?

Kate Transchel, "Why a $3 Bottle of Vodka Won't Cut It," Globalpost.com, January 18, 2010. Reprinted by permission.

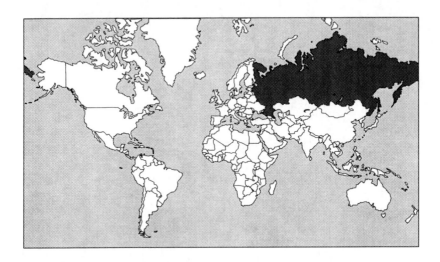

Russian President Dmitry Medvedev is apparently under the impression that curing his country of its alcohol problem has a price—and that price is $3 a bottle.

On Jan. 1 [2010], a new law in Russia took effect that sets minimum prices for vodka. Now, the cheapest half-liter bottle costs 89 rubles ($3), nearly double what it cost previously. According to media reports at the time of its launch, the new law was meant to protect the health of Russians as well as curb the black market sale of imitation vodka that is often made with shoddy and harmful ingredients.

But in reality, the new law is a Band-Aid solution at best. Like many other such misguided efforts that have been tried in Russia, it doesn't address the root of the problem: how hardwired Russian society is for drinking.

Russia's Love of Drinking

Consuming on average 32 pints of pure alcohol per person per year, Russians are among the heaviest drinkers in the industrialized world. Their love of alcohol dates back more than a thousand years. In 986, Grand Prince Vladimir is said to have declared, "Drinking is the joy of Russia. We cannot do without it," and adopted Christianity as the official religion of Russia supposedly because it was the only one that had no prohibition against drink.

Over the last several hundred years, alcohol has crept into the social, political and economic fabric of everyday life. As one 19th-century commentator put it: "When the Russian is born, when he marries or dies, when he goes to court or is reconciled, when he makes a new acquaintance or parts from an old friend, when he negotiates a purchase or sale, realizes a profit or suffers a loss—every activity is copiously baptized with vodka." However hyperbolic this assessment might be, it is true that alcohol lubricates nearly every social interaction among ordinary Russians, including and especially at work. In fact, a nationwide study conducted in 1991 found that Russians drank more at work than at home or in bars.

The state benefits tremendously from the average Russian's attachment to drinking. Since the first appearance of taverns in Moscow in the 16th century, the Russian state has attempted to exercise political and fiscal control over the trade in spirits, ultimately establishing a monopoly over the production and sale of alcohol. By the end of the 19th century, alcohol revenues comprised about 40 percent of all state revenue.

Over the last several hundred years, alcohol has crept into the social, political and economic fabric of everyday life.

The Long-Standing Russian Dilemma

And herein lies Medvedev's dilemma: how to continue reaping the tremendous taxes gained from alcohol sales while also trying to reduce alcohol consumption (or appearing to try to do so). It is a dilemma every Russian leader has faced since the 19th century. And nearly every leader over the last hundred

"Skeleton in the Desert," cartoon by Alexei Talimonov, www.CartoonStock.com. Copyright © by Alexei Talimonov. Reproduction rights obtainable from www.Cartoon Stock.com. Reproduced by permission.

years has attempted to foster popular temperance to ill effect. (An exception is Boris Yeltsin, who notoriously got drunk and drove his car into the Moscow River, or wandered the streets of Washington, D.C., in his underwear.)

The first all-out effort by the state to combat drinking was in 1914, when Tsar Nicholas II implemented prohibition as part of Russia's mobilization for World War I—six years before the 18th Amendment made America "dry." He figured the best way to get peasants to the front was to get them there sober.

The result was that moonshine (samogon), which had not been widely consumed, became epidemic. Bootlegging used up precious stores of grain needed to feed the troops. Some scholars even argue that by depriving the state of desperately needed alcohol revenues at the outset of the war, prohibition exacerbated the state's decline and precipitated the Bolshevik revolution in 1917.

An Escalating Problem

Once the dust settled, following WWI, revolution and civil war, Joseph Stalin made a decision to reintroduce the state's liquor monopoly, citing the need for revenue to rebuild the country and industrialize. He simultaneously launched an aggressive anti-alcohol campaign that included propaganda, price controls and a system of incentives and punishments. But even with all the state's resources at their command, the Bolsheviks failed to create a sober workforce. Workers rebelled, moonshine spread and ultimately the state abandoned the campaign and purged all its leaders.

In fact, after each anti-alcohol campaign that was tried after Stalin—by Nikita Khrushchev, then Leonid Brezhnev—the level of alcohol consumption in the country nearly doubled. In 1966, the state introduced a series of fines for public intoxication, and established a network of labor rehabilitation centers. Despite these repeated efforts, state alcohol output increased and per-capita consumption steadily rose throughout the 1960s and 1970s.

Mikhail Gorbachev made combating alcoholism a top priority when he became leader in 1982. He restricted alcohol sales, reduced production by 50 percent, created a nationwide temperance society and prohibited alcohol consumption in many public places. The results were disastrous: sugar, used in the production of moonshine, disappeared from stores; vast numbers of people poisoned themselves with other intoxicants such as brake fluid and rubbing alcohol; and the government lost nearly 2 billion rubles in alcohol revenues.

A Failed Campaign

The population became angered by the abrupt unavailability of alcohol and some people took to drugs. During these years, the number of people treated for alcoholism declined by 29 percent. At the same time, the number of drug addicts more than doubled.

Gorbachev's failed temperance campaign cost him a tremendous amount of popularity and support—and that cost isn't something Medvedev is willing to pay. To address alcoholism in a responsible way, by investing in the long, hard slog of education and behavioral change, is a road most politicians shy away from. Medvedev's feeble attempts are largely political, because any serious attempt to deal with alcohol abuse in Russia would cost a lot of money and would take a serious bite out of state revenues.

If history is any indication, the new law raising vodka prices will also prove to be futile—alternative drinks and bootleg whiskey will flood the market.

When Medvedev began his war on alcoholism in August 2009, he launched a remarkably short-sighted campaign encouraging young people to drink beer over vodka. The level of beer drinking rose considerably, but vodka consumption remained the same. Now, the state is burdened with the task of undoing that campaign's messages on top of everything else.

If history is any indication, the new law raising vodka prices will also prove to be futile—alternative drinks and bootleg whiskey will flood the market. The problem isn't cheap alcohol, or its availability. The problem lies much deeper than that, and solving it would cost far more than $3 a bottle.

The British Should Not Allow Alcohol Companies in Health Policy Talks

Anna Gilmore and Jeff Collin

Anna Gilmore is a professor of public health at the University of Bath, and Jeff Collin is director of the Global Public Health Unit at Edinburgh University. In the following viewpoint, they criticize the British government's decision to invite leading food and alcohol companies to partner with the government to address the country's growing alcohol and obesity epidemics. Gilmore and Collin maintain that these companies are increasingly viewed as vectors of disease and should not be allowed a seat at the table when it comes to public health policy. Such companies, they argue, will lobby for ineffective and voluntary initiatives that will not impact their profitability.

As you read, consider the following questions:

1. According to the authors, what did Andrew Lansley promise to food and alcohol companies in exchange for funding?
2. What tactics do the authors think that food, alcohol, and tobacco companies use to sell their products and influence regulators?
3. What do the authors see as the prime motivation of food, alcohol, and tobacco companies?

Anna Gilmore and Jeff Collin, "Drinks Companies Spread Liver Disease as Surely as Mosquitoes Do Malaria," Guardian.co.uk, February 21, 2011. Reprinted by permission.

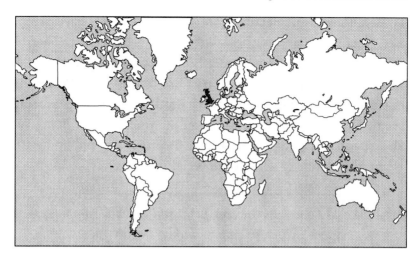

Alarm bells rang in the public health community when Andrew Lansley [the UK secretary of state for health] announced last summer [in 2010] that leading food and alcohol companies were being invited to join a "partnership" with government to help address the obesity and alcohol epidemics. As further details of the Public Health Responsibility Deal for alcohol emerge, much through investigative work by the *Guardian*, the bells ring ever louder.

The Public Health Responsibility Deal

The Public Health Responsibility Deal, part of the government's "big society" idea, is just one of several such deals. For alcohol and obesity, it brings together large numbers of food and alcohol company representatives with far fewer government and public health representatives in a series of "networks" charged with encouraging and enabling consumers to adopt better diets and drink sensibly. However, full details of their function or how they relate to broader public health policies have yet to emerge.

The health secretary originally suggested that in return for providing funding these companies could expect "non-regulatory approaches". It is now becoming clear, for alcohol at least, that Lansley could more straightforwardly have promised "ineffective approaches". Policies known to reduce harmful alcohol use have apparently been precluded from the deal, while those with negligible impact are central to it. While the government's announcement of minimum alcohol pricing seemed more promising, the level at which this is being set also suggests limited commitment to protecting public health where this conflicts with commercial interests.

While the government sees food and alcohol companies as partners in health policy, public health increasingly recognises them as vectors of disease.

The United Kingdom's Most Serious Health Problems

The products of food and alcohol companies are, alongside tobacco, responsible for this country's ... most serious public health problems. Britain now has one of the highest obesity rates in Europe, while alcohol misuse costs over £17bn each year. Whereas rates of tobacco use are falling in the UK, obesity and alcohol use have barely begun to be addressed. Those hoping that we could finally build on progress with tobacco to effectively tackle the alcohol and obesity epidemics will be as disappointed as the corporate sector is delighted.

While the government sees food and alcohol companies as partners in health policy, public health increasingly recognises them as vectors of disease. The vector concept, adapted from infectious disease control, is simple: Liver disease and myriad other health and social problems are being spread by alcohol companies just as the mosquito vector spreads malaria. The conduct of these corporate vectors should therefore be studied and where necessary countered just as we study and control the mosquito to reduce deaths from malaria.

The Tobacco Vector

Understanding of the tobacco industry vector is much further advanced than food or alcohol thanks to millions of internal documents tobacco companies were forced to release through litigation. Evidence of industry misconduct revealed in these documents has driven serious legislative efforts to combat its attempts to undermine public health. The tobacco industry is now more tightly regulated and its conflicts of interest with public health actively managed.

It is no coincidence that the marked reductions in tobacco use in this country (a 25% fall over the last decade) and progress in tobacco control globally have coincided with an increase in regulation and the tobacco industry's gradual exclusion from the policy arena.

A Prime Opportunity for Food and Alcohol Companies

The broader lessons from tobacco control are apparently not being learnt. A recent WHO [World Health Organization] report noted how the tobacco industry had long been "demanding a seat at government negotiating tables, promoting voluntary regulation instead of legislation . . . gaining favour by financing government initiatives on other health issues". Yet for the alcohol and food industries, such engagement constitutes the government's preferred model of policy making. The deal seemingly delivers Diageo, SABMiller, McDonald's, PepsiCo, Mars UK and others privileged access via which to push their preferred voluntary initiatives. It also appears they have been invited to contribute to government health campaigns that could carry their logo—the sort of brand-stretching and credibility-enhancing opportunity of which companies dream.

Can partnerships with alcohol and food companies justifiably form the basis of public health policy? Tactics used by major food and alcohol companies to sell their products and influence their regulatory environment closely mirror those of the tobacco industry. These include focusing on personal responsibility, claiming government intervention infringes individual liberty, vilifying critics, working to undermine studies contrary to their interests, supporting ineffective educational programmes and voluntary codes that help preclude binding regulation. Food, alcohol and tobacco companies have also worked collaboratively to preclude effective public health policies and share youth marketing tactics. This is perhaps not surprising—Philip Morris (now Altria, the world's largest tobacco transnational) until recently owned Miller Brewing Company and Kraft Foods and the revolving door between these companies appears well used.

Profitability vs. Social Responsibility

It is entirely unsurprising then to find the food and alcohol industries adopting such positions. Corporations, whether they sell tobacco, food or alcohol, are legally obliged to maximise shareholder revenue. Their social responsibility is to pursue economic growth rather than health promotion or environmental protection. It is therefore effectively incumbent upon them to oppose any policies that could reduce profitability. Evidence shows that pushing ineffective voluntary measures, like those being mooted in the deal for alcohol, is key to securing this objective.

If the deal fails to significantly address the obesity and alcohol epidemics, the blame will lie with government. It has apparently declined to recognise the fundamental conflicts of interest involved when corporations are invited to design policies ostensibly aimed towards reducing harmful behaviours on which their profitability depends. The deal seems underpinned by presumptions rejecting policies known to work and promoting those that don't. In short, information now emerging on the "responsibility deal" for alcohol suggests it will be entirely consistent with industry preferences and incapable of effectively addressing one of the UK's most serious public health problems.

There may be a case for collaboration or negotiation with business in implementing specific measures, but this requires careful scrutiny and management of the conflict between commercial interests and core public health goals. The government can generate funds while simultaneously addressing the alcohol epidemic, but it should do so via what is known to work—raising taxes—rather than by education campaigns in conjunction with industry. Committing to partnerships in which necessary measures are excluded from discussion and ineffective voluntary agreements are promoted would suggest that the government's approach might be better termed an "irresponsibility deal".

Periodical and Internet Sources Bibliography

The following articles have been selected to supplement the diverse views presented in this chapter.

| Bruce Crumley | "French Combat Youth Binge-Drinking," *Time*, July 17, 2008. |

Kate Dailey — "Women and Whiskey: Why Not?," *Newsweek*, December 24, 2010.

Stuart Elliott — "F.T.C. to Take Another Look at Alcohol Ads," *New York Times*, March 8, 2011.

Elise Jordan — "Karzai's Nightlife Crackdown," The Daily Beast, May 15, 2010. www.thedailybeast.com.

Daniel Ten Kate — "Thais Get Sober Message: Ban Liquor Ads," *Christian Science Monitor*, December 5, 2006.

Andrei Litvinov — "Medvedev's Anti-Alcohol Campaign Tries to Make Russia Sober Up," *Newsweek*, September 4, 2009.

Catherine Mayer — "Nation O'Drinkers: Scotland Takes on Alcohol Abuse," *Time*, March 5, 2009.

Vivienne Nathanson — "Alcohol Is Costing Us Dearly—We Need Action Now," *Guardian*, March 14, 2011.

Eric Pfanner — "France Weighs Big Changes in Drinking Laws," *New York Times*, October 28, 2008.

Randeep Ramesh — "Binge Drinking: Only One Measure Can Solve Our Drink Problem," *Observer*, June 5, 2010.

Frances Schwartzkopff — "Alcoholics May Stop at One Drink with Help from Lundbeck Anti-Abuse Drug," Bloomberg.com, December 23, 2010. www.bloomberg.com.

GLOBAL VIEWPOINTS

CHAPTER 3

Religion and Alcohol

Alcohol Ban Aside, Wine Industry Thrives in Morocco

Alfred de Montesquiou

Alfred de Montesquiou is a reporter for the Associated Press. In the following viewpoint, he finds that Morocco's wine industry is thriving despite the Islamic ban on alcohol consumption for Muslims. In fact, he contends, Morocco is ranked as one of the largest winemakers in the Muslim world, and the industry contributes much-needed tax revenue, provides employment, and supports the country's important tourist industry. The author maintains that although there have been some Islamic protests, the country continues to show a tolerance toward the wine industry as well as toward alcohol consumption.

As you read, consider the following questions:

1. How many millions of bottles of wine were produced in Morocco in 2008?
2. According to the author, how much wine does a Moroccan drink every year on average?
3. For how many years does the author say that Morocco has made wine?

Meknes, Morocco—The gently rolling hills planted thick with vineyards are an unlikely sight for a Muslim country partly set in the deserts and palms of North Africa. Yet the

Alfred de Montesquiou, "Alcohol Ban Aside, Wine Industry Thrives in Morocco," Associated Press/*Richmond Times-Dispatch*, April 18, 2009. Reprinted by permission.

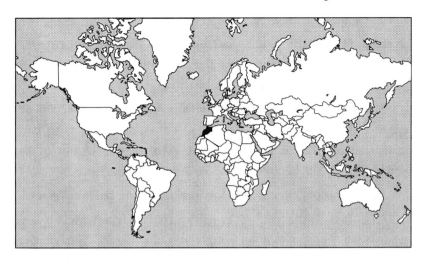

grapes, and the wine they produce, are thriving in Morocco despite Islam's ban on alcohol consumption.

Morocco has become one of the largest winemakers in the Muslim world, with the equivalent of 35 million bottles produced last year. Wine brings the state millions in sales tax, even though Islam appears to be on the rise politically.

"Morocco is a country of tolerance," said Mehdi Bouchaara, the deputy general manager at the Les Celliers de Meknes, the country's largest winemaker, which bottles over 85 percent of national output. "It's everybody's personal choice whether to drink or not."

Statistics . . . show that Moroccans consume on average 1 liter (a quarter of a gallon) of wine per person each year.

The Celliers have flourished on this tolerance. The firm now cultivates 2,100 hectares (5,189 acres) of vineyards, bottling anything from entry-level table wine to homemade champagne and even a high-end claret, Chateau Roslane, aged in a vaulted cellar packed with oak barrels imported from France. The winery now dwarfs virtually any other producer in Europe.

On paper, wine is "haram," or forbidden to Muslims. But Bouchaara said the firm's distribution is all legal since it only sells to traders authorized by the state, who in turn officially sell exclusively to non-Muslim tourists.

Statistics, however, show that Moroccans consume on average 1 liter (a quarter of a gallon) of wine per person each year, and the Moroccan state itself is the largest owner of the country's 12,000 hectares (29,652 acres) of vineyards.

The paradox illustrates Morocco's delicate balancing act.

The fast-modernizing country thrives on tourism and trade with Europe, but its people remain deeply conservative. The country's ruler, King Mohammed VI, is also "commander of the believers" and protector of the faith. Islamists authorized to take part in politics are the second-largest force in parliament, while support for non-authorized groups is believed to be even larger.

Despite this uncertain setting for wine culture, the Celliers' owner, Brahim Zniber, is one of the country's richest people. His group employs 6,500 people, nearly all of them Muslim, and revenues rose to 225 million euros last year. Its three biggest sources of income are wine production with the Les Celliers de Meknes, hard liquor imports and Coca-Cola bottling.

Zniber's latest ventures include the new Moroccan champagne and plans to build a luxury hotel offering the country's first "vinotherapy" spa resort, with health care creams and baths based on grape products. But the group has also tested the limits of the gray zone it operates in. The "wine festival" it helped promote in 2007 caused protests in nearby Meknes, a deeply religious city of 500,000 run until recently by an Islamist mayor.

"The festival was an unnecessary provocation," said Aboubakr Belkora, the former mayor who was slammed by his own Islamist group, the Justice and Development Party, for halfheartedly authorizing the gathering in the town.

Changing Fortunes of the Moroccan Wine Industry

The heyday of Moroccan wine was the French colonial era. At its peak in the 1950s, the country had 55,000ha (hectares) of vineyards, producing 3 million hectolitres a year, mainly so-called *vins médicins* for beefing up anaemic French wines. At independence, Morocco lost most of its wine-making expertise, its consumers and its main export market. By the 1990s, the vineyard area had dwindled to 8,000ha. King Hassan began Morocco's wine renaissance in the 1990s by attracting French investors who planted new vines and transformed quality. Wine is now big business.

Rupert Joy, "Moroccan Wine and Muslims,"
Decanter.com, June 6, 2008. www.decanter.com.

Elected in 2003, Belkora was removed this past January by the Interior Ministry because of allegations of mismanagement and graft. He denies the accusations, saying they were politically motivated. Belkora doesn't think he was punished because of the wine festival, but views authorities as wary of the Islamists' growing political clout.

"They don't want us to be too successful," he contended, noting that the administration picked his replacement from outside Islamist ranks.

The ex-mayor said that "for religious reasons," he uprooted about 100 hectares (247 acres) of vineyards from his own fields but has no qualms with others making or drinking wine.

"There has always been an acceptance in Morocco, for wine, for homosexuality . . . you just don't need to advertise it," he said in an interview.

Others find there is some hypocrisy to the practice.

Hassan, a restaurant manager, who did not provide his last name, said he wasn't allowed a license to serve alcoholic drinks because he is Muslim. "But everyone knows we serve wine with our food," he said, pointing at the restaurant's patrons, both foreign and Moroccan, sipping their wine over dinner.

Another owner in Meknes, who also requested anonymity because of his practices, said he served wine in tinted glasses, kept bottles out of sight and told clients to say they were drinking soft drinks if questioned. "Police rarely come, and if they do they never look inside the glass," he said. These practices reflect a much more lenient culture than in other Muslim countries.

Alcohol is completely forbidden in hard-line Iran or Saudi Arabia. In Sudan, offenders regularly get sentenced to lashings in court. Even in nearby Algeria, another large wine producer, alcohol consumption is fast shrinking to just the capital and a few exclusive tourist resorts.

Within Morocco's more favorable context, the Celliers winery sells 27 million bottles per year, mostly in Morocco. Two million bottles head to Europe or the United States. The firm is planting another 800 hectares (1,977 acres) of grapes to meet new demand from China, said Jean-Pierre Dehut, a former liquor-store owner in Belgium hired as the Celliers' export manager.

By the size of the huge new bottling plant it is building and the 450 people it employs, the Celliers is more on par with the new, industrial-scaled wine businesses in Australia, Chile or California than with Europe's often family-owned domains. But Dehut stressed that Morocco has made wine for at least 2,500 years, since the Phoenicians colonized its coast. "This country exported wine to Rome during the Roman Empire," he said.

Kurdish Club Scene Booms as Baghdad Bans Alcohol

Associated Press

The Associated Press (AP) is a news organization. In the following viewpoint, AP describes a booming nightclub scene in the Kurdish region north of Iraq after a harsh crackdown on liquor in the south. Baghdad, once the capital of Middle East nightlife, has come under the sway of Islamic officials and activists who are intent on banning liquor. As a result, a number of musicians, dancers, and impresarios are migrating to Kurdish areas to take advantage of more tolerant laws and attitudes.

As you read, consider the following questions:

1. When did the alcohol crackdown in Baghdad begin, according to the Associated Press?
2. How many licenses were granted for clubs and bars in Kurdistan in January 2011?
3. From where do most of the women working in Kurdish nightclubs hail, according to the Associated Press?

*I*raqis head north to party as club scene in Baghdad, once the capital of Middle East nightlife, dries up after official crackdown on liquor.

Dozens of men gathered in the smoky little club to watch five scantily clad dancers sway their hips to the beat of a drum

Associated Press, "Kurdish Club Scene Booms as Baghdad Bans Alcohol," Associated Press/*Jerusalem Post*, January 11, 2011. Reprinted by permission.

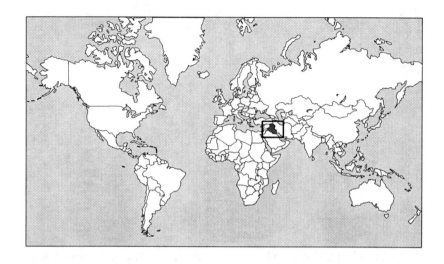

and the grooves of an electric piano. Once a common sight in Iraq's capital, Baghdad, the scene can now only be found in the more liberal Kurdish north.

Dozens of dance halls and clubs have opened across the Kurdish region during the past months, capitalizing on a crackdown against alcohol in Baghdad, where officials in November began closing clubs serving booze and banned alcohol sales at stores.

That prompted the capital's nightlife—its musicians, dancers and impresarios, and the patrons who flock to them—to migrate north.

"Baghdad has become a dead city where there is no more amusement, no drinks and no music. They have dressed the capital in religious clothes," said Hameed Saleh, a Baghdad academy of music graduate who plays the drums and oud, the Arabic forerunner to the lute, at Kurdonia Club. "Now I play music in Sulaymaniyah and my life is secure."

Baghdad in the 1970s and 1980s was renowned for being the capital of Middle East nightlife with the most raucous nightclubs and an endless flow of whiskey. UN sanctions and Saddam Hussein's newfound piety dimmed its star a bit in the

1990s, but it was the U.S.-led invasion in 2003, the violence that ensued and the rise of conservative Islamic militias that all but snuffed it out.

Nightlife in Baghdad tried to rise from the dead after violence declined in 2008, but the final blow came when religious conservatives began enforcing a Saddam-era ban on alcohol in clubs and added a ban in stores.

Now artists and entertainers have joined the refugees who over the past seven years streamed from other parts of Iraq into the three provinces that make up the Kurdish autonomous region in the north, seeking a safe haven from violence.

At the Love Club in Sulaymaniyah, Muhanad Hamad, a 26-year-old trader from the city of Tikrit, 80 miles (130 kilometers) north of Baghdad, was showering one of the singers with wads of cash.

Nightlife in Baghdad tried to rise from the dead after violence declined in 2008, but the final blow came when religious conservatives began enforcing a Saddam-era ban on alcohol in clubs and added a ban in stores.

"This is the only place in Iraq where I can enjoy my personal freedom and seek joy far from security worries. Nobody can question me about what I am doing," he said.

Many of the clients in these places hail from Baghdad and other provinces to the south, said club owner Haithem al-Jabouri, himself from Baghdad. He picked Sulaymaniyah to open his club in November because it's so much more secure than the rest of Iraq.

It was security that also drew Raghad Abdul-Wahab to the city. The 26-year-old used to dance at clubs in one of Baghdad's wealthier neighborhoods but religious leaders near her home tried to convince her family it was immoral. She always felt unsafe when she would leave the club in the evening, and then when Baghdad officials turned off the alcohol, she decided to move north.

American Soldiers and Moonshine in Iraq

Despite the ban on all alcoholic beverages and strict Islamic prohibitions against drinking and drug use, liquor—Iraqi moonshine in particular—is cheap and easy to find for soldiers looking to deal with the effects of combat stress, depression or the frustrations of extended deployments, said military defense lawyers, commanders and doctors who treat soldiers' emotional problems.

Paul von Zielbauer,
"In Iraq, American Military Finds It Has an Alcohol Problem,"
New York Times, *March 12, 2007.*

"I am free here, and I can dance as I like. I just do my job and I get some money," she said.

The Kurdish government's tourism department has given licenses to at least 10 clubs and bars in the province over the last month, said Mustafa Hama Raheem, director of the licenses office in the tourism department. Many more clubs have opened in people's homes or private buildings without licenses, he said.

He said the clubs and dance halls are a boost for the local economy.

"We have to attract tourists to stay for a longer time here and our young men who used to travel to other countries seeking their personal freedoms," he said.

The clientele is a mixture of Kurds and people who come from the rest of Iraq for entertainment, he said. The women are mostly from Baghdad, Basra and some southern provinces. Many of them went to places such as Syria and the United Arab Emirates in 2006 and 2007 but returned to work when things became safer in Iraq.

The nightlife boom has not been to everyone's liking.

An imam at a mosque in Sulaymaniyah, Hamza Shashoi, said the government should be more concerned with addressing issues like unemployment among young people than opening clubs that promote vice.

"Opening the nightclubs is very risky. . . . We are a Muslim society," he said.

But the difference between Baghdad and Sulaymaniyah is that those religious beliefs don't dictate society's rules for everyone, said a spokesman for the Kurdish ministry of religious affairs, Meriwan Naqshbandi.

"In the Kurdish region, the clerics or religious men have no role in the government of the region, they cannot exercise any pressure on the government's resolutions," he said.

Until nightclubs can once again freely operate in Baghdad, artists and dancers like 23-year-old Muna Maad will stay in Kurdistan. One recent night she was dancing among a group of young men, her eyes lined darkly with black eyeliner and wearing a short white skirt. Periodically the men would slip Iraqi dinars into her tight white shirt in a show of appreciation.

It's a long way from a moment six months ago in Baghdad, when a group of gunmen raided the dance hall where she was working.

"When they found us dancing they insulted us . . . and forced us to leave," she said, adding "I will not return to a place where no rules and laws exist."

Afghanistan's Islamic-Influenced Alcohol Regulations Create a Booming Underground Market

Sayed Yaqub Ibrahimi

Sayed Yaqub Ibrahimi is a staff reporter for the Institute for War & Peace Reporting. In the following viewpoint, he finds that tougher restrictions on alcohol imports have created a boom for the Afghan moonshine industry. Although alcohol is forbidden by Islam, it is popular with many Afghanis, especially young men, and authorities have been largely ineffective in dealing with the problem. A number of homemade alcohol producers use foreign bottles to package their moonshine, because it appeals to status-conscious consumers.

As you read, consider the following questions:

1. What does the author say nearly killed off the moonshine industry in Afghanistan in 2001?

2. According to General Khalil Anderabi, how many bottles of imported alcohol were confiscated in Faryab, Afghanistan?

3. How old is the wine-making business in Afghanistan?

The label may say "Stolichnaya" but the contents of this vodka bottle have never seen Russia. Instead, it is a potent local brew made from raisins, which is keeping many a party going in northern Afghanistan.

Sayed Yaqub Ibrahimi, "Afghan Moonshine a Growth Industry," Institute for War & Peace Reporting, August 27, 2008. Reprinted by permission.

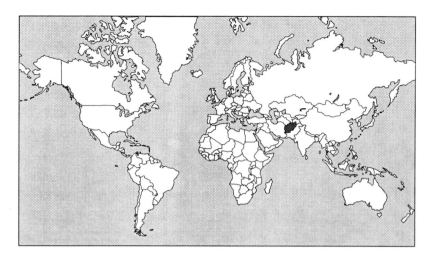

Pahlavan Omar—not his real name—owns a small distillery in the northern city of Shiberghan, where he produces alcohol along with his two young sons.

The distillery is not much to look at—just a few barrels, some sacks of raisins, a couple of pressure cookers and stoves.

But according to Pahlavan, business is booming.

"Over the past few months, our production has doubled and our customers are coming back," he said.

Alcohol is forbidden by Islam, and the ban was strictly enforced when the hard-line Taliban regime held sway in Afghanistan.

The Impact of Alcohol Imports

Neither religious precepts nor fundamentalist rulers stopped this illicit industry. Instead, what nearly put paid to it was the relaxation of restrictions on alcohol imports that followed the collapse of the Taliban regime in 2001.

"The Taliban would have hanged us if they had known about it, but we continued producing, although at a lower rate, when they were around," said Pahlavan. "It was when Afghanistan opened its doors to foreign products and prices fell that we had to close down most of our distilleries."

About two years ago, however, the Afghan government tightened the rules on alcohol imports, and the flow of foreign liquor dried up. Afghan tipplers once again had to seek out the local suppliers.

Pahlavan smiled broadly, saying, "The government was not trying to give our business a boost, but in any case it was a great help to us."

The Resurgence of Afghan Moonshine

He produces 20 litres of vodka a week in his small distillery. He buys leftover raisins from markets or wholesalers, paying about 500 afghani, some ten US dollars, for a 50-kilogram sack. He steeps them in water for about a week and brews up the resulting mixture in a pressure cooker. The steam is siphoned off and cools into the final product, raw spirit.

According to aficionados, Afghan moonshine contains a high percentage of alcohol—though quite how much is hard to determine, and differs from batch to batch. But consumers say it is more than enough to do the job.

"We produce about ten litres of alcohol from each barrel," explained Pahlavan. "We package it in plastic bags and sell it to shops."

According to aficionados, Afghan moonshine contains a high percentage of alcohol—though quite how much is hard to determine, and differs from batch to batch.

The drink sells for about 500 afghani a litre, so that the return on each sack of raisins is about 5,000 afghani, or 100 US dollars—ten times the initial investment.

As Pahlavan's business grows, he is selling more and more of his product wholesale to shopkeepers, even though this nets him only 400 afghani a litre.

Market and Packaging Moonshine

Imaginative marketing can increase the returns. One entrepreneur in the northwestern town of Maimana imports empty Russian vodka bottles from Pakistan and uses them to make his product more attractive to customers.

"Afghanistan's vodka is the best, but now people are used to these foreign bottles. We have to imitate them to make more money," he said.

This producer sells his "vodka" for 1,000 afghani a bottle—about 20 dollars.

"The quality of our vodka is much higher than the foreign one. We were producing and drinking it when there was no foreign alcohol in Afghanistan," he said.

Shopkeepers confirm that it is easier to sell the "Russian" brand.

"People don't want to buy alcohol in plastic bags," said one shopkeeper in Mazar-e-Sharif. "It makes no difference to us—we make twice as much in profits."

Alcohol Laws in Afghanistan

The production, sale, and consumption of alcohol are forbidden by law in Afghanistan, and officials insist offenders will be punished.

But the producers appear unabashed—given the all-pervasive ubiquitous corruption in this country, it should not be hard to get police to look the other way.

General Khalilullah Aminzada, provincial police chief in Jowzjan province, said that his forces have closed down approximately ten distilleries since the beginning of 2008, and have jailed the offenders.

However, he acknowledged that there are many more that the authorities are unaware of.

"This is a major social problem," he told IWPR [Institute for War & Peace Reporting]. "This is nothing new—alcohol production has a very long history in Afghanistan. These problems will continue as long as societies exist, and our struggle against them will also continue."

Wily Entrepreneurs

General Khalil Anderabi, the police chief for the neighbouring Faryab province, admitted that his region was home to numerous distilleries and that so far he has not been able to close a single one.

"We have recently learned that there are such establishments in the province," he told IWPR. "It is against the law and we have a specific plan to shut them down, but they are very artful."

Instead, said Anderabi, police in Faryab have concentrated on imported alcohol, confiscating about 1,200 bottles so far from shops.

Although plentiful, alcohol is not on public display.

"Now we will begin to battle these domestic producers, and we will stop them," he said.

Although plentiful, alcohol is not on public display. A recent informal survey carried out by IWPR reporters showed that many shopkeepers will not sell to people they do not know, denying they have supplies even when they themselves are obviously inebriated.

Alcohol and Young Afghanis

Alcohol consumption is on the rise in northern Afghanistan, particularly among young men who use it to spice up parties or to dull the frustration of unemployment.

Mohammad Qais, from Shiberghan, works for an international organization and is an avid consumer of homemade vodka.

"When we go on picnics on Fridays we always take a bottle or two," he told IWPR. "Without alcohol we wouldn't enjoy our parties."

An Islamic Backlash

Others, however, frown on drinking as a violation of Islamic values.

Sadruddin, a taxi driver in Kabul, said, "Every day I pick up one or two passengers who are drunk. It was never like this in the past. Drinking alcohol is very common now. There are no parties without vodka.

"This is not a good thing. Young people should know that it is contrary to Islam."

Religious scholars also condemn the practice, and warn that punishment awaits those who imbibe.

"If the alcohol user repents, God may forgive him," said Qari Hayatullah, a religious scholar in Mazar-e-Sharif. "If not, he leaves the world a sinner, and he will be punished in the afterlife."

In this life, though, the religious scholars cannot agree on the penalty for alcohol use.

"There is a difference of opinion among religious scholars as to the punishment for the producer and user of alcohol," said Qari Hayatullah. "It is not like murder or adultery; the punishment is not specified."

Under the Taliban, those who were caught using alcohol had their faces blackened with soot and were paraded around the city as a lesson to others.

Alcohol for Personal Consumption

Because of the continuing prohibition, some farmers restrict themselves to making alcohol only for their own consumption.

"I produce my own vodka, which is unique in all the world," said one vineyard owner in Sar-e-Pul. "I don't care about the high price of imported alcohol, or the restrictions on production and use. I make it because it's delicious. I set aside the best grapes and produce enough alcohol to last a year. The taste of this homemade vodka is better than the best European alcohol."

This man pointed out that aside from distilling vodka, wine-making is a centuries-old tradition that predates Islam in Afghanistan.

Many people age their vodka like whiskey, to give it a deeper flavour. Besides, as the Afghan saying goes, "Old wine makes for a special kind of intoxication."

Qatar Is Willing to Make Concessions on Alcohol Ban for 2022 World Cup

Alexander Smoltczyk

Alexander Smoltczyk is a correspondent for Der Spiegel. *In the following viewpoint, he outlines Qatar's successful push to host the 2022 World Cup that has caused an uproar with many fans concerned about the country's strict alcohol laws. Currently, only Qatari luxury hotels serve alcohol. During the games, the government will create party zones, where fans can buy and consume alcohol. Some officials hope that the games will facilitate an open discussion of Islam for Western countries and clear up misunderstandings about Muslim societies.*

As you read, consider the following questions:

1. How many people are living in relative proximity to Qatar, according to the author?
2. What natural resource does the author say that Qatar has in abundance?
3. Where is Qatar's national soccer team ranked?

S hortly before the delegation from football's international governing body FIFA [Fédération Internationale de Football Association] left Doha [the capital city of Qatar] on Sept.

Alexander Smoltczyk, "Qatar Has High Hopes for 2022 World Cup," spiegel.de, December 15, 2010. Reprinted by permission.

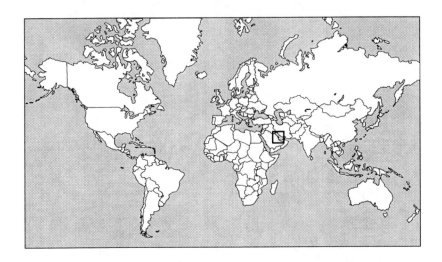

16 [2010], it was invited to a presentation in a pavilion. The cool, windowless room, furnished with cube-shaped leather armchairs and with lounge music playing on the sound system, could just as easily have been in Madrid or New York.

Atkon, a Berlin-based event planning firm, had spent months working on the 39-minute show that was now unfolding in front of the FIFA experts, complete with 3-D technology and surround sound. Laughing children and wise sheikhs swirled across the screens, stadiums grew and the camera zoomed in to show images from the past and the future. There was even a daring simulation of an imaginary WM opening match, in which Qatar beats Germany 2:0. In one scene, Deutsche Bahn [AG] CEO Rüdiger Grube appeared on a yellow cloud and said, in somewhat broken English, that he was keeping his fingers crossed for Qatar.

It was all so convincing, attractive and real. When French football legend Zinédine Zidane appeared in the corner of the room after the presentation, the FIFA team thought he was a hologram at first.

The booming emirates on the Gulf are known for their elaborate 3-D presentations. Their rulers are crazy about the technology. And they have the money to turn simulations into reality.

As of Dec. 2 [2010], it is now clear that in 12 years' time, the soccer World Cup will take place in the desert nation of Qatar, a country that has never participated in a World Cup. The German tabloid *Bild* called it a "Qatarstrophe" while the Norwegian newspaper *Dagbladet* described FIFA's decision as "the biggest football joke of all time." It was a scandal for everyone who sees football as a game for Europe and its former colonies.

Football, it seems, is leaving home.

Not Just Dominos

"So what?" says Uli Stielike. "It's time we realized that they don't just play dominos in the Orient." Stielike, a former footballer who played on the German national side that were runners-up in the 1982 World Cup, is sitting with his wife in a Starbucks café in the City Center mall in Doha.

He is the latest former German national player to have found work in Qatar recently. Famous German footballers Stefan Effenberg and Mario Basler played briefly in Qatar, collected a million or two, then left again. Stielike has been a coach in Qatar for the last two years. He currently trains the Al-Sailiya team and plans to renew his contract.

His team usually plays for a crowd of about 300 fans. Going to football matches hasn't quite caught on among Qataris, who prefer to watch games on television, he says. "But that will change completely when there's a World Cup involved," says Stielike. "Nowhere are there so many sporting facilities per capita than in Qatar. The rulers here are the biggest fans. They all play football themselves."

Qatar lies in the heart of geopolitical darkness, located at almost exactly the intersection of imaginary lines extending from Afghanistan to Sudan, and from Iran to Yemen. FIFA may have had its own, obscure reasons for choosing Qatar. There are also good reasons to stage something other than a clash of civilizations in this afflicted part of the world for a change. "There is one thing people haven't understood," says Stielike. "The World Cup wasn't awarded to Qatar, but to an entire region."

More precisely, he is referring to the Tropic of Cancer, the zone circling the globe that extends from Mexico through Mauretania to Taiwan, a region that is home to many of the migrant workers who spend every day creating wealth in the Gulf. The Gulf's population of 146 million people includes at least 17 million foreigners from every country imaginable. If we include Jordan, Syria and Egypt, societies that are no less enthusiastic about soccer, there are 260 million people living in relative proximity to Qatar.

Anything can take place anywhere provided there is enough money and the airports have been expanded as needed.

The Gulf Overtakes the West

The Gulf, one of the world's most globalized regions, is home to Indian investment bankers, British port logistics experts and German petroleum geologists, Iranian exiles, refugees from Sudan and Yemen, fortune seekers from Birmingham and entire clans from South India, Afghanistan, Syria and Egypt. It ought to be enough to fill the stadiums.

"In a very short amount of time, the Persian Gulf has became a collector of civilizations without parallel," the German philosopher Peter Sloterdijk concluded during a visit to the region. The West has lost its monopoly on art collections like those of the Louvre and the Guggenheim. And since the decision by Zürich-based FIFA, it has also forfeited its monopoly on its holy of holies, the World Cup. The tournament is going where everything goes, it is following the money and following in the footsteps of the Formula 1 [auto racing] circus, cycling, tennis and golf.

Place and event have become disconnected. Anything can take place anywhere, provided there is enough money and the airports have been expanded as needed. The International Monetary Fund has predicted 16 percent growth for the Qatari economy in 2010. No economy in the world is growing at a faster pace.

The government is considering expanding the area where alcohol consumption is permitted for the duration of the World Cup.

Rules Will Be Relaxed During the World Cup

The Islamic cultural center Fanar stands on Doha's Corniche waterfront promenade, beyond the skyscraper construction sites. Its tower, spiraling into the pale sky, is designed to give "humanity a guiding light." Ahmed Ijas, the director of the center, suggested that deeply religious people book a trip to Mecca during the weeks of the World Cup. Ijas says that his remark was misunderstood, and adds: "We are pleased that the World Cup is coming to Qatar." It's just that certain rules will have to be observed, he points out.

Doha's luxury hotels have been serving alcohol for a long time. The government is considering expanding the area where alcohol consumption is permitted for the duration of the World Cup. For four weeks, the holy Koran will be suspended in specially marked "fan zones," where beer and bratwurst will be served. This is what FIFA expects from Qatar.

One of the party zones is in Al-Rumaila Park, within sight of the Fanar center. Ijas doesn't have a problem with this. "Islam doesn't prohibit men from taking their shirts off. But they should be covered from the navel to the knees." But Ijas, who lived in England for many years, knows that after 16 pints, few fans can tell where their navels or knees are.

The country's clerics seem to have adjusted to the idea of being lenient for four weeks. There had been concerns over how Sheikh Yusuf al-Qaradawi would react to the FIFA decision. The president of the International Union of Muslim Scholars lives in Doha and is known as a hard-liner and an anti-Semite. But in his Friday prayer, the sheikh expressed his delight over the World Cup decision—even after the ruling family had made it clear that a team from Israel, complete with its fans, would also be welcome.

Qatar's overall level or counterterrorism cooperation with the United States is "considered the worst in the region," the US State Department writes in one of the leaked embassy cables. But Qatar is one of the Arab countries that have issued visas to Israeli athletes, including 3,000-meter runner Yosef Gezachew, who attended the [International Association of Athletics Federation] World Indoor Track & Field Championships in Doha in March.

If it goes well, "Qatar 2022" could trigger a wave of modernization throughout the region by the time the first match begins.

Too Much Cash

Allah has given the faithful of this tiny nation one of the world's largest reserves of natural gas. This is an even more attractive asset than oil wealth, because liquid gas burns more cleanly than oil, and demand is expected to grow.

Qatar has only one problem: What to do with its money. Qatar Holding, a subsidiary of one of the world's largest sovereign wealth funds, already owns Harrods, the London high-end department store, and parts of Volkswagen. The Qatar Foundation will soon be advertising on the jerseys of FC Barcelona, a deal which will cost it €165 million between now and 2016.

Qatari Youth and Alcohol

Consumption of alcohol is likely to be largely ignored by the country's predominantly young population, as it is swept away with the euphoria of hosting the competition [referring to Qatar's hosting of the 2022 World Cup], many believe.

"Around 50 to 60 percent of the population are aged in their 20s or below, so they are more tolerant and I think they will embrace the event as a whole," said Sultan al-Qassemi, an Emirati social commentator based in the United Arab Emirates.

Regan E. Doherty,
"2022 World Cup Presents Challenge for Tiny Qatar,"
FoxNews.com, December 15, 2010. www.foxnews.com.

Last week [December 2010], the German construction company HOCHTIEF announced that the Qataris would acquire about 10 percent of its shares. As a result of the investment, it is clear that HOCHTIEF will be building most of the World Cup stadiums and the world's longest link between countries, a bridge from Qatar to the island nation of Bahrain.

Deutsche Bahn AG, the German national railway, has been awarded the contract to build Doha's new 320-kilometer metro system, and a southwestern German company will apparently supply the air-conditioning systems for the World Cup stadiums.

As an exporting nation, Germany stands to make more money on the desert World Cup than it did on its own World Cup in 2006. Qatar's bid book, weighing in at five kilograms (11 pounds), was the work of the Frankfurt architecture firm

Albert Speer & Partners and two German project development companies. Speer has designed eight of the nine new stadiums. If it goes well, "Qatar 2022" could trigger a wave of modernization throughout the region by the time the first match begins.

Don't Bet on Qatar Being Eliminated

The Aspire Zone sports complex on the outskirts of Doha includes the Khalifa [International] Stadium, performance laboratories, a sports clinic, the Aspire Mosque, a swimming pool and a towering hotel that looks like an Olympic torch. It also has the world's largest covered sports arena, which cost $1 billion alone. It took less than 22 months to build the entire complex on the desert floor.

For Qatar's ruling family, the al-Thanis, Aspire is its strongest asset in the international business of sports. Financially strapped national teams, the Iraqis, for example, can train there for free. Since 2004, talented young football players have been trained there on a global scale. Most are Qataris and other local residents, but 5 percent are scholarship holders, mainly from Africa. The facility's 300 experts come from 60 countries, and there is also a branch in Senegal.

Andreas Bleicher is the sports director at the Aspire academy. A native of Germany's southwestern Swabia region, Bleicher once headed the German Olympic base in Leverkusen near Cologne. "I wouldn't bet on Qatar's team being eliminated in the group round in 2022," he says. "A player who got started five years ago as an eight-year-old will be of an ideal age by then."

Qatar pays for "Football Dreams," a worldwide talent-search program. Bleicher objects to the charge that the program is merely an excuse for Qatar to snap up African talent. "The boys have all gone back to their countries, where they are now playing on the under-17 teams in Ghana, Mali and the Ivory Coast," he says. The program generates goodwill for Qatar, which translates into votes in the relevant committees.

A Dream World Cup for Fans

Bleicher feels that the decision by FIFA and its president, Sepp Blatter, to "embark on new paths" is inevitable. "The opposing arguments are just outrageous. The United States and South Africa don't allow people to walk down the street with bottles of liquor in their hands. In Qatar, it will be possible, for the first time, to see several matches in one day, because every-thing will be reachable by metro or water taxi. This will be a dream World Cup for fans."

For Bleicher, the reactions are evidence of wounded egos and prejudice. "The World Cup can help improve the discussion of Islam and immigration in Germany. People will have to take a closer look at these things." It is hard to predict, says Bleicher, the many ways this decision could affect the Middle East.

Bleicher gazes at the empty, carefully designed world in front of the entrance to his academy. It's 28 degrees Celsius (82 degrees Fahrenheit) outside, ideal football weather. Then he says: "It couldn't be taken into account during the application process. But now, of course, one could consider moving the tournament to the winter." A decision could hinge on the cooperation of the powerful leagues in Spain and England, which have no winter breaks. "2022 is still a long way off. But that has to come from FIFA."

Earning the World Cup

Qatar's national team is currently ranked 113th in the world. According to FIFA rules, the host country's team automatically qualifies for the tournament, even if the team has never even qualified to play in a single World Cup. For Qatar, the rule was its only chance to ever be allowed to play in the tournament—a $4 billion ticket.

Venga Rajish, who is from India, believes that the price is appropriate. Rajish delivers groceries for a living. He is standing in front of Tawfeeqs Cool Stores, across the street from the Fanar center, with his fellow workers from Syria and China. He says that he will definitely take his sons to the World Cup, even if he is living in his native Kerala again by then. He is "coming back," he says.

Kerala, a state in southwestern India, would not be able to afford to build expensive stadiums. Rajish worked in Bahrain for 10 years and has been working in Qatar for three years. He works seven days a week, and is too busy to go to the stadium on Fridays.

But he loves football, he says. Almost as much as cricket, he adds. "We have earned the World Cup," says Rajish.

Periodical and Internet Sources Bibliography

The following articles have been selected to supplement the diverse views presented in this chapter.

David Ariosto   "Illegal Alcohol Destroyed in Kabul, Officials Say," CNN.com, July 22, 2011. www.cnn.com.

BBC News   "Muslim Integration 'Easier in Scotland than England,'" August 9, 2010.

Robert Duncan   "Libya: Tippling, Tires, Tripoli, Tyrants, and a Tree (Part One)," Renew America, July 11, 2007. www.renewamerica.com.

Economist   "Kurdistan Diary: Mountains and Waterfalls," July 11, 2008.

Lucy Fleming   "Sudan's Date-Gin Brewers Thrive Despite Sharia," BBC News, April 29, 2010.

Erik German   "Moroccan Winemaker Thrives," GlobalPost, February 3, 2010. www.globalpost.com.

Simeon Kerr   "Alcohol Producers See Cheer in Region," *Financial Times*, January 3, 2011.

Qassim Khidhir   "Alcohol Sales Booming in Kurdistan," *Kurdish Globe*, November 15, 2009.

Brian Murphy   "Saudi Arabia Partying: Elite, Boozy and Secret," *Huffington Post*, December 8, 2010.

Anjana Sankar   "Illegal Residents in UAE Turn to Alcohol," *Gulf News*, July 26, 2010.

Alex Spillius   "WikiLeaks: The Raucous Underground Lifestyle of Young Saudi Royals," *Telegraph*, December 8, 2010.

Habib Toumi   "Kuwait Denies Report It Will Lift Alcohol Ban," *Gulf News*, November 3, 2010.

GLOBALVIEWPOINTS

CHAPTER 4

Alcohol Culture and Tradition

Britain's Campaign for Real Ale Is a Way to Preserve Traditional Pub Culture

Leah McLaren

Leah McLaren is a contributor to Maclean's. *In the following viewpoint, she reports on the British Campaign for Real Ale, which is a movement to appreciate and advocate for traditional ales and preserve the country's rich drinking culture. Proponents of the campaign also hope to lower the rates of binge drinking that have been escalating in recent years and foster a sense of community spirit that many people believe has been lost in the younger generation.*

As you read, consider the following questions:

1. According to McLaren, how many traditional pubs close in Britain every week?
2. What ratio of British adults drink over the safe alcohol limit at least once a week, according to the Office for National Statistics?
3. By how much has Tesco increased its selection of ales since 2005?

Once a year at the Old Spot pub in Dursley, Gloucestershire, barman Steve Herbert hosts a beer tasting for graduating students at the village school. He calls it finishing

Leah McLaren, "How to Solve Britain's Problems? Ale," macleans.ca, September 30, 2010. Reprinted by permission.

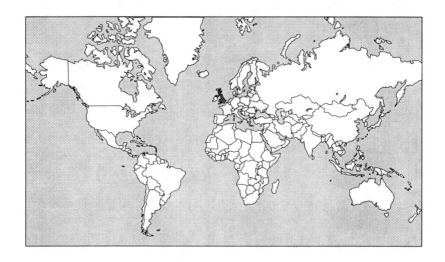

school for sixth formers. "The point is to get them off the fizzy, sweet stuff before they head off to university," he explains, "so they don't end up rushing into pubs, drinking shots and throwing up all over themselves."

The Campaign for Real Ale

Welcome to Britain's Campaign for Real Ale [CAMRA]—a growing movement to preserve the traditional drinking habits of a culture whose relationship with alcohol is as historied as it is confounding. For years, Britain has seen the decline of local pubs. At present, 39 traditional boozers close each week. At the same time, binge drinking—and its attendant hooliganism—is on the rise. According to the most recent study conducted by Britain's Office for National Statistics, more than a third of adults drink over the safe alcohol limit at least once a week.

What's the solution to this cultural conundrum? According to a growing number of Britons, the answer may be fermenting at the bottom of a traditional cask of local ale.

Ales, commonly known as "bitter" in England, are the old-fashioned bitter beers best known for being served at room temperature to toothless men in rural pubs. They are brewed in the traditional way, using warm fermentation, which, with the addition of hops, produces a strong, herbal flavour to offset the sweetness of malted barley. Lagers, on the other hand, are brewed using modern refrigeration to produce a milder and arguably less complex flavour.

Welcome to Britain's Campaign for Real Ale—a growing movement to preserve the traditional drinking habits of a culture whose relationship with alcohol is as historied as it is confounding.

Campaign Results

For decades, ales have lived in the shadow of their modern counterpart. But now, according to the British Beer & Pub Association, traditional ale's market share nudged up 0.2 percentage points from the year before to claim 20.6 per cent of the overall market, while lager slipped by 1.2 points to 74.3 per cent overall. In a country where lager still predominates, the boost is the first gain for ale makers in generations. It also comes at a time when retailers are reporting increases in demand for ales. Tesco, the nation's biggest off-licence retailer, has increased its selection of ales from 20 to 350 since 2005.

But will this slow resurgence of yeasty hops and malt be enough to save a traditional drinking culture in decline? Jonathan Mail, the head of policy and public affairs for the consumer advocacy group Campaign for Real Ale (CAMRA), hopes so. In his view, traditional pubs and ales are intrinsically linked in British culture: "You can't campaign for one without campaigning for the other."

This is because the people who are abandoning pubs for cheaper, more processed forms of alcoholic entertainment tend to be lager drinkers rather than imbibers of handmade, local cask-fermented traditional ales. Real ale (or "craft beer," as it's known among draft snobs) cannot be mass-marketed to

"Campaign for Real Ale," cartoon by Dave Parker, www.CartoonStock.com. Copyright © by Dave Parker. Reproduction rights obtainable from www.CartoonStock.com. Reproduced by permission.

trendy nightclubs or widely distributed in supermarkets, which makes it an excellent draw for the neighbourhood watering hole.

Recent Campaign Events

In the past several months, the campaign to save traditional ales and pubs has heated up across Britain. CAMRA currently boasts a membership of over 120,000, and late last year [2009]

Britons watched a five-part reality series *Save Our Boozer*, which featured a handsome Yorkshire barman helping rural communities to restore and run their flagging locales. London journalist Kate Burt, meanwhile, has started a blog to save local pubs (www.savetheboozer.blogspot.com). She describes her mission in cultural terms: Old boozers, she said in an interview, are Britain's "only remaining hope of engendering good old-fashioned community spirit that spans cultures, age, gender, persuasion, and class."

Last year, the then minister of public health condemned alcohol consumption as one of the country's "most challenging public health issues," and the British Medical Association called for an official ban on all alcohol advertising. Drinkaware, an organization funded by alcohol producers and retailers like Tesco and Waitrose, also launched a $160-million drive to highlight the dangers of alcohol misuse. But the government crackdown—largely in the form of stiff tax levies—may have inadvertently contributed to the nation's drinking problem. By sharply increasing the duty on beer—now roughly 80 cents per pint—the government has ensured the downfall of many small pubs. Local watering holes like the Old Spot can no longer compete with nightclubs or grocery chains, many of whom carry cheap beer and wine as a loss leader.

The result? Fewer kids having a quiet pint of ale with gran at the local on a Saturday night, and more Jägerbomb-related stabbings on the high street.

That's why Steve Herbert believes that the resurgence of traditional craft ale, which can only be sold from casks behind the bar, may be the answer for pubs—and Britain. "A fresh, local product promotes thoughtful drinking," he says. "We're trying to send the message that pubs are about having drink and a chat, not a place to get completely slaughtered."

Japan Needs a Broad Educational Program to Change Alcohol Culture

Eric Johnston

Eric Johnston is a staff writer at the Japan Times. *In the following viewpoint, he reports that the alcohol abuse problem is extensive in Japan. Johnston points to a lack of public awareness and education on the issue of alcohol abuse and finds that most Japanese see it as a social problem, not as a disease that requires treatment. Many people believe that there needs to be a big change in public attitudes before the country's alcohol problem is effectively addressed.*

As you read, consider the following questions:

1. What important public figure in Japan was treated for alcoholism in July 2007, according to the author?
2. How many specialized centers for the treatment of alcoholism does the author say there are in the country?
3. According to health official Susumu Higuchi, how many people in Japan fit the clinical definition of alcoholic?

He seems to have it all. A tenured university professor in the Kansai region, fluent in English and partially conversant in Chinese, he is consulted by senior local business lead-

Eric Johnston, "Alcoholism Remains a Taboo Issue," japantimes.co.jp, April 17, 2009. Reprinted by permission.

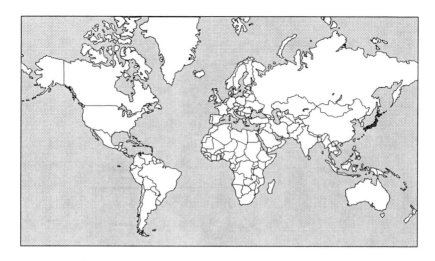

ers seeking advice on doing business in the United States and Europe and has served on local government committees promoting international exchanges.

But the professor, who didn't want his name revealed, has a secret—he's an alcoholic. His addiction has nearly cost him his secure university position, forced him to cancel media appearances and, once, prevented his attendance at a conference in Paris, where he was due to deliver a keynote speech.

"Alcoholism is a disease. But Japanese society as a whole still doesn't see it that way, and few people I work with know that I'm an alcoholic," the 63-year-old educator said, adding he attends a Kansai chapter of Alcoholics Anonymous.

Japanese Drinking Culture

"The pressure to drink, either for business or social reasons, remains strong, especially among members of my generation. Heavy drinkers are admired for their strength and forgiven for their rude behavior, which is ignored the next day," he said.

"In July 2007, Prince Tomohito was treated for alcoholism. The eldest son of Prince Mikasa and Princess Yuriko, he was long known for having alcohol problems. But his public admission was a surprise to many and of some concern to some in the Imperial Household Agency who worried about a negative public reaction," he added.

On the other hand, former Finance Minister Shoichi Nakagawa's problems with alcohol, which resulted in his resignation after an allegedly drunken appearance at a press conference in Italy, won little sympathy from the public.

Media reports indicated that politicians, bureaucrats and media elements who cover the Nagata-cho political center had known for years Nakagawa was a heavy drinker. But whereas Prince Tomohito finally admitted he had a problem and needed help, Nakagawa was unable to do so until he publicly embarrassed Japan.

Attitudes Toward Alcoholism in Japan

Kurihama National Hospital in Kanagawa Prefecture, where Prince Tomohito sought treatment, opened the country's first specialized ward for alcohol abuse in 1963. It is now Japan's leading institution for treating alcohol addiction and one of 10 specialized treatment centers nationwide. In fiscal 2008, the center treated 1,195 new patients, while another 16,548 were repeat visitors.

Susumu Higuchi, deputy director of National Hospital [Organization] Kurihama Alcoholism Center, said there has been little change in basic public attitudes toward alcoholism during the past couple of decades, with most Japanese seeing it is as a social problem rather than a disease requiring medical treatment. At the same time, there appears to be less consumption of alcohol than in the past.

"Laws against drunk driving have toughened over the past decade or so, as people recognize the dangers of drinking before you get behind the wheel," Higuchi said. "Overall, those in large cities like Tokyo and Osaka are drinking less than in the past.

"At the same time, certain groups, including women in their 20s, often drink heavily, while many members of the baby boom generation, which is now retiring in record numbers, find themselves out of work and with time and money on their hands to do more drinking," he added.

The Challenge of Raising Public Awareness

Doctors and nongovernmental organizations involved in helping those with alcohol problems note public education campaigns and programs have had limited effect in raising awareness.

In 1992, the then Education Ministry ordered all schools to teach the harmful effects of alcohol in health education classes, but by 2002, according to a follow-up survey, less than half of those polled knew what the signs of alcoholism are.

Doctors and nongovernmental organizations involved in helping those with alcohol problems note public education campaigns and programs have had limited effect in raising awareness.

The Alcohol Problem in Japan

A survey presented by Higuchi in February [2009] revealed how extensive alcohol abuse is in Japan. Higuchi estimated that in fiscal 2003, people aged 15 and above on average consumed about 7.7 liters of alcohol annually. Nearly 8.6 million people consumed more than 60 grams of alcohol daily, which is considered excessive.

Higuchi estimated there were 800,000 people who fit the clinical definition of an alcoholic and a further 4.4 million suspected of being alcoholics.

Symptoms of alcoholism include a strong desire to drink; an increased tolerance that leads to greater consumption; an inability to control one's intake; ignoring other pastimes; and continuing to drink, despite knowing it is the cause of various psychological and personal problems.

If someone displayed at least three of these symptoms over the past year, or more than three symptoms at the same time within a one-month period, they would be considered alcoholics in need of treatment.

Public Policy Issues

As to Japan's public policy regarding alcohol, there are warning labels on alcoholic beverages and restrictions on advertising them. But these are largely voluntary measures, and Higuchi noted there are no legal restrictions on TV ads, although many of those who advertise on TV have created essentially voluntary restrictions.

Alcohol is not legally available to minors, in other words to those under 20. But there are no restrictions on small shops that sell liquor. Nor, as in certain U.S. states, are there restrictions on the times or days of the week when booze can be sold.

The Kansai professor agreed less advertising and some restrictions on alcohol sales may at least help deter heavy drinking. But what is first needed is broader public education and public sympathy for those who suffer from alcoholism, he said.

Higuchi noted that although Prince Tomohito's admission and Nakagawa's problems made headlines, they did little to change basic attitudes. Still, he added, the right kind of public figure can often take the lead in changing public perception.

"In America, (the late) President Gerald Ford's wife, Betty, admitted she was an alcoholic, and her admission won her lots of sympathy, started a serious public health debate about alcoholism, which helped make it less taboo, and led to the creation of the Betty Ford clinic for alcoholics," Higuchi said.

"That hasn't happened in Japan yet," he added.

Workplace Drinking Culture Takes Growing Toll

Lee Ho-jeong

Lee Ho-jeong is a staff writer for Korea JoongAng Daily. *In the following viewpoint, she maintains that the integral role of excessive drinking in Korean corporate culture is having major economic, health, and social effects on workers. It is particularly hard on women, who often feel pressured to take part in binge drinking sessions with their colleagues. Workers who do not drink or decline to participate in such sessions often find themselves discriminated against and ostracized.*

As you read, consider the following questions:

1. According to the Ministry of Health and Welfare, how many Koreans suffer from physical problems caused by excessive alcohol consumption?
2. According to a JobKorea/Bizmon survey, what percentage of female employees in Korea drink heavily at least once a week?
3. According to Chung Woo-jin, what is the economic loss caused by drinking every year in Korea?

Drinking among Korean employees costs the economy trillions of won and is damaging people's health at a growing rate, according to private companies, government departments and university researchers.

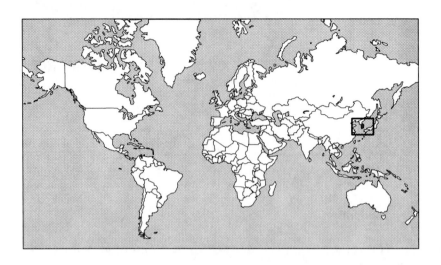

"In this country 2.2 million people are suffering from physical disorders caused by alcohol consumption, including alcohol addiction," said Lee Won-hee, an official at the Ministry of Health and Welfare.

A recent survey by Yonsei University showed that Korea loses almost 1.5 trillion won ($1.7 billion) per annum as a result of alcohol abuse, a figure that's 50 percent higher than in Japan.

A new survey of almost 5,000 office workers, conducted by the recruitment consultants Job Korea and Bizmon, found that 83.5 percent of those questioned drank significant amounts more than twice a week, and of those, almost 50 percent had difficulty working the next day.

"Drinking has become a bigger social and economic problem than smoking," said Chung Woo-jin, a social welfare professor at Yonsei University who helped produce the school's study of alcohol's damaging effects. "Drinking destroys families, causes disease and death and promotes suicide, which is an enormous loss to the country."

Korea has the highest suicide rate among OECD countries.

Women are increasingly becoming victims of the drink culture, as they begin to occupy more prominent roles in the workplace and are expected to participate in binge drinking sessions with male colleagues.

Several women told the *Korea JoongAng Daily* that they had been coerced by colleagues, usually senior executives, into drinking more than they wanted. Some said they had left jobs because they found the drinking culture too extreme or because they'd been harassed.

Women are increasingly becoming victims of the drink culture, as they begin to occupy more prominent roles in the workplace and are expected to participate in binge drinking sessions with male colleagues.

"Women, in adapting to the work environment, are having to smoke and drink more to be accepted, and many women find this very hard," Chung said.

Last Tuesday, a 32-year-old employee of a major conglomerate returned home at 2 a.m., following a drinking session with his co-workers. Less than six hours later he was at his desk with a bad hangover, which interfered with his work all day.

"I felt nauseous and constantly barfed air," said the man, who asked to be known as Lee. "I had a hard time concentrating."

This is not the first time Lee has felt this way. Like many other Korean workers, Lee drinks at least twice a week with people from his office.

The drinking sessions that Lee attended are typical of thousands which take place every week.

In Lee's case he would start at half past six and go on until midnight, at least. Once a week he is obliged to drink with senior executives and, on these occasions, copious amounts of beer, soju and whiskey are consumed.

"When you're drinking with your boss, it's hard to refuse, especially when you consider your future."

Although Lee is well aware that drinking will make him sick, he says it's hard to quit.

Drinking is a part of Korea's corporate culture. Despite overwhelming evidence about the dangers of alcohol abuse, many Korean companies see binge drinking as a key aspect of team building and those who do not drink can face criticism and end up being ostracized.

"Koreans, especially men, believe that drinking helps strengthen companionship," said Lee. "They think drinking sessions improve communication between colleagues."

Lee hopes that he and his co-workers might find other ways to strengthen their team spirit, such as hiking, or going to the movies.

"But drinking is what most people do," he said. "And it is all they will always do."

Lee is among many Koreans who have grown tired of the nation's drink culture. At a recent orientation course for a government department the drinking was so heavy that one employee had to be hospitalized.

"I was horrified," said an employee who witnessed the events and was interviewed on condition of anonymity. "One senior executive said people who don't drink should be fired."

One dangerous development is the number of women who are being cajoled into taking part in binge drinking.

The JobKorea/Bizmon survey revealed that almost 40 percent of female employees now drink heavily at least once a week and anecdotal evidence suggests the development is causing unhappiness among many women.

At a private conglomerate, one of the biggest in Korea, young women are expected to drink boilermakers, a potent mix of whiskey and beer, in drinking competitions, until they are unable to stand.

"I felt the drinking was mandatory," said an employee, a young management trainee who left a good job at the company after a harassment incident that took place during a drinking session.

"I did not want to drink so much but it was forced upon us by superiors," she said. "The worst thing was that the chief executive was leading everybody else in making us drink."

A young woman who did not want to be identified and works for a government-funded corporation had a similar experience.

"My superiors forced me to drink boilermakers and I hated it," she said.

"The superiors love it when the women drink more."

As females become more prominent in the workforce, and assume more responsibility, their reluctance to drink will clash more frequently with traditional male values.

Foreign visitors to Korea often express surprise about the number of drunk office workers who crowd the streets on weekdays, a sight that is almost unheard of in New York or London, where excessive drinking is seen as something that damages team spirit.

At a recent interview for a management consultancy job, a well-qualified applicant with a doctorate in her field, who does not want to reveal her identity, told the interviewer that she did not drink. The man, an executive, said that her answer was "disappointing."

Foreign visitors to Korea often express surprise about the number of drunk office workers who crowd the streets on weekdays, a sight that is almost unheard of in New York or London, where excessive drinking is seen as something that damages team spirit.

But in Seoul, during the week, it is common to see a group of inebriated men in suits trying to hail a cab or staggering past a row of brightly lit bars.

The Job Korea/Bizmon survey of 4,878 office workers found that 38.9 percent of its respondents drank two or three times a week and 7.6 percent drank more than four times a week.

Forty-three percent of men drank two or three times a week. In addition, 43.7 percent of the poll said they consumed alcohol at office parties, while 23.4 percent said they drank because of social meetings. Twenty-three percent said they drank to relieve stress.

Health problems are a significant issue. Forty-four percent said they had experienced deteriorating health as a side effect of alcohol consumption.

Additionally 27.3 percent said drinking had caused financial problems.

However, 29.5 percent said they thought drinking helped their business, but only 15.6 percent said drinking increased solidarity within organizations.

These numbers paint a stark picture. While many Korean companies admit they use drinking parties for team building, less than one-quarter of their employees think it's an effective technique and almost half believe it has damaged their health or productivity.

In some countries, including the United States, companies that make alcohol have been compelled to warn their customers about the risks of heavy drinking. Korea has been heading in the opposite direction.

Soju, Korea's most popular drink, had one of its best years in 2006. Sales grew at the fastest pace since 2001 with a 6 percent increase over 2005.

Jinro, Korea's biggest soju producer, with an 80 percent market share, sold 3.2 billion bottles, but it has no separate budget set aside to educate the public about the dangers of drinking and, since 2001, it has stopped making donations to alcohol addiction treatment centers.

The company's public relations office cited bad business in the last half decade to explain why the treatment and education programs had been stopped.

The economic damage caused by heavy drinking was demonstrated in a study by Chung Woo-jin, a social welfare professor at Yonsei University.

Every year, the economic loss caused by drinking, including diminished productivity, is around 1.5 trillion won ($1.7 billion), which represents 2.86 percent of Korea's gross domestic product.

This is far more than Japan's 1.9 percent, Canada's 1.09 and France's 1.42. Loss of productivity accounts for 42 percent, or 6.3 trillion won. Loss due to death caused by drinking accounted for nearly 30 percent (4.5 trillion won). Alcohol-related diseases accounted for 6 percent, or 909.1 billion won.

Property loss due to accidents resulting from alcohol consumption accounted for 1.6 percent, or 244.4 billion won.

In a separate study of 72,964 patients diagnosed with liver cancer, released in 2004 by the National Health Insurance Corporation, those who drank more than 1 bottle of soju at least three days a week were 8.2 times more likely to get liver cancer.

Cho Surnggiei, a researcher at the Korean Alcohol Research Foundation, believes that the current drinking culture is unlikely to change soon.

"In fact the number of women drinking alcohol in this country has increased as more women have become active in the workplace," Cho said. "Everybody knows that excessive drinking leads to productivity losses and health problems but, unlike Western countries where excessive drinking is believed to be bad for business, Koreans think that it helps business relations."

A Korean Work Outing

A typical hoesik, or company outing, in Korea starts at a grilled meat restaurant, where work colleagues wash down their food with soju. Afterward, the group usually goes to icha (a second round), oftentimes a bar. Samcha (third round) usually involves a Korean karaoke bar, where boiler-makers of whiskey and beer are offered. Those who survive the third round go onto a fourth round, which often involves haejangguk, or hangover soup, accompanied by more beer or soju.

Cho Jae-eun, "Bottoms Up?
Corporate Korea Distorts Historic Drinking Culture,"
Korea JoongAng Daily, February 23, 2011.

Cho said the drinking culture began when the Korean economy started to grow in the 1970s. Before then alcohol wasn't easily accessible to most people.

In the beginning, when companies were smaller and more intimate, superiors bought drinks for their employees because they had the bigger paycheck. The purpose of drinking was to boost morale and to make it easier to control staff.

"When drinking, people become irrational," said Cho. "It becomes easier to control the will of employees when they become alcohol dependent."

By the 1980s, when the nation was under military rule, the drinking culture that's common today began to take shape, as military practices were incorporated into the workplace.

The mandatory acceptance, by junior staff, of drinks poured by their seniors comes from this time.

As business flourished, companies started to set aside separate budgets that could be used to buy alcohol for employees.

"In Western culture alcohol is considered to be a substance that is addictive and dangerous. In Korea it is seen as a bridge that connects people," Cho said. "Younger office workers are trying to find alternatives to drinking, such as going to concerts or exhibitions but groups like these are limited."

Many researchers say it will be hard to change Korea's drinking culture but experts say some small steps would help.

"Drinking a little alcohol to strengthen a relationship among co-workers is not evil in itself," said Cho. "What is bad is that 50 percent drink excessive amounts and feel they must keep drinking, even when they want to stop. Nobody should be forced to drink, period."

The research foundation offers guidelines that it believes can limit the damage, the most important of which is that nobody should try to make others drink.

The research foundation also runs various campaigns that promote alternatives to drinking such as lectures and gallery visits.

Last week the foundation presented a lecture on the negative effects of excessive alcohol consumption to employees at a plant in the Siheung Industrial Complex, Gyeonggi province.

Some companies have begun to chose an alternative to guzzling down boilermakers on weeknights.

Victor Kye, the former public relations manager of the LG Arts Center, said his employees, the majority of whom are women, go to concerts and other cultural events instead of drinking soju.

"It is a pleasant change," Kye said. "After watching the performances the team goes for tea or a glass of wine and we talk about what we have just seen."

Kye's experience is a rare example. For the most part, Korean office workers feel harassed and intimidated by the country's drinking culture.

A management official at a government ministry, who wants to be known as Lim, recently explained to a supervisor at a party that drinking was impossible for her because of a medical condition.

"He became angry," said Lim. "He shouted that nobody had refused a drink in the first round for 50 years. He would not stop complaining about it. He made me feel bad."

Germany's Beer Culture Is in Decline

Christian DeBenedetti

Christian DeBenedetti is a journalist specializing in travel and craft-beer subjects. In the following viewpoint, he investigates the decline of the German beer industry. DeBenedetti attributes the diminishing popularity of German beer to an archaic purity law that dictates ingredients used in the brewing process; this law has stifled innovation in Germany while the rest of the world is experimenting and moving forward. There are signs, however, that with recent changes to the law and a few groundbreaking collaborations the German beer industry is reviving and evolving.

As you read, consider the following questions:

1. According to German federal statistics, when is the last time German brewing production has been as low as it was in 2011?
2. How many breweries are there in Germany today?
3. According to the author, how many common styles are used for brewing in Germany?

Germans, famously, coin neologisms when a crisis hits or the culture reels in a new direction. Take *die bad bank* (toxic lender), *kreditklemme* (credit crunch), or *twittern*

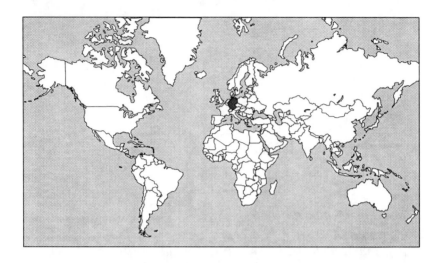

(sending a message via Twitter). Because Germany's brewing industry has fallen on hard times, especially since the mid-1990s, you'll now hear *brauereisterben* (literally, "brewery death") muttered across the land as well. That may sound a little ridiculous, but in a country practically synonymous with beer and brewing—buxom servers in dirndls and overflowing steins, the *biergarten* echoing with song—the possibility of a downturn is a major buzzkill.

An Industry in Decline

The facts are stark: According to German federal statistics released in late January [2011], German brewing has dropped to less than 100 million hectoliters of production for the first time since reunification in 1990. (That's less than half of the United States' annual output.) The same study revealed that consumption dropped almost 3 percent last year alone, to 101.8 liters per person per year, and that it's down about one-third overall since the previous generation. The number of breweries in the country has also dropped—by about half over the last few decades to around 1,300. (There are nearly 1,700 up and running in the U.S.) The vaunted Weihenstephan brew master degree program in Munich adopts a dour tone on its student prospectus, saying the majority of graduates don't actually become brewmasters but instead head for jobs in mechanical engineering and the chemical and pharmaceutical industries.

The Rise of the United States

Further evidence of *brauereisterben* is depressingly easy to pile on. Berlin, which sustained some 700 breweries in the early 19th century, now counts only about a dozen firms. Amid the ruins, highly trained German brewmasters are giving up and heading to the United States—even to sleepy Covington, La., where Henryk Orlik, a graduate of Munich's prestigious Doemens Academy, settled down in 1994. "I came here for the great American craft-beer industry," the Heiner Brau founder told me recently over samples of freshly brewed pilsner in his charming little brew house just off the town square. Adding insult to injury, craft brewers in the United States have largely taken over the prestigious international-brewing awards circuit. Sierra Nevada Brewing Co., founded 30 years ago by home brewer Ken Grossman in Chico, Calif., took top honors in a hotly contested 2010 World Beer Cup category, besting 68 other brands, many of them German. The bracket? German-style pilsner.

Assessing the Industry

These days, Germany's celebrated brewing towns and atmospheric old taverns can feel like retirement homes. Visitors to the south of Germany today (where more than half the nation's breweries are located) find few of the ardent young beer lovers that crowd craft watering holes in Copenhagen; Brussels; London; New York; Portland, Ore.; and even Rome. And while it's true that last fall's 200th Oktoberfest was bigger than ever, using Oktoberfest to measure the health of German beer culture is like using Disney World admissions to measure the health of American cinema. Once a decorous wedding pageant, Oktoberfest is a hot mess, with cheesy carnival rides and hordes chugging cheap lager as if it were Hawaiian Punch. Paris Hilton even showed up for the anniversary celebration.

It's also true that there are still a lot of small German breweries that produce great beers worth seeking out, from juicy, clovey Bavarian *hefeweizen* and bready *ungespundet-hefetrüb* (unfiltered lager) to the malty *altbiers* of Düsseldorf and the grassy, refreshing *kölsch* beers of Cologne. In Bamberg (north of Munich, in the area historically known as Franconia), distinctive smoked beers called *rauchbier* predominate, and the most steadfast craft-beer lovers will make the pilgrimage to taste these specialties. In 1997 I spent three happy months in Germany studying ancient brewing techniques on a Thomas J. Watson Fellowship and came away deeply impressed by the idyllic places where traditional brewing has survived the 20th century's punishing economies of scale. But some of the same breweries I visited that year have already closed, and I can scarcely imagine the variety that would have existed had I visited just half a century earlier.

These days, Germany's celebrated brewing towns and atmospheric old taverns can feel like retirement homes.

Reasons for the Decline

German beer–industry spokesmen are quick to blame the downturn on the nation's declining birth rate and aging population—if there were more teenagers and twentysomethings, the logic goes, there'd be more beer drinking. But the fact is that bored young Germans are abandoning the entire alcoholic genre of beer itself. They're flocking to mixed and energy drinks like Bacardi's Rigo and Austria's amped-up export, Red Bull, whose sales surged 18 percent in Germany during 2009.

A more likely culprit for the *brauereisterben* is the country's very definition of beer. Germany's brewing industry has, for nearly 500 years now, marched under the banner of the *Reinheitsgebot* (literally, "purity commandment"). A law enacted in 1516 to control prices and shield the baking industry from supply shortages by excluding rye and wheat from brewing, the *Reinheitsgebot* stipulated that beer must contain only malted barley, hops, and water (wheat and yeast were written in later). The decree—often described as the world's first consumer protection legislation—dried up the ancient pre-hops tradition of *Gruitbier*, which likely included yarrow, bog myrtle, juniper, rosemary, mugwort, and woodruff—all perfectly useful bittering and flavoring plants. It also pulled the plug on *Köttbusser*, an ancient brew made with oats, honey, and molasses. While the *Reinheitsgebot* was actually overturned in 1987 as an impediment to European free trade, many German companies adhere to it for marketing purposes, especially in Bavaria. When it comes to beer for local consumers (exports are mostly brewed without the strictures), it's still the *de facto* law of the land.

Initially, the *Reinheitsgebot* improved the state of German (and, by extension, worldwide) beer quality immensely and helped make Germany's brewers world famous for quality. No one wants to go back to the Dark Ages when beer was murky, dark, sour, and smoky, sometimes fattened up with roots, bone, ash, or squawking fowl.

The fact is that bored young Germans are abandoning the entire alcoholic genre of beer itself.

An Archaic Law Stifles Innovation

Trouble is, the *Reinheitsgebot* is now working against the very industry it was supposed to preserve. For one, it puts a vise grip on innovation by demonizing flavor- or body-enhancing additions of any kind: oats, ancient grains (such as spelt, millet, and sorghum), spices, herbs, honey, flowers other than hops, and any other natural fermentable starches and sugars.

This taboo rules out trying Belgian, French, and New World brewing styles, which often call for re-fermentation in the bottle with sugar in a manner similar to champagne.

Technically, when the *Reinheitsgebot* was officially replaced in 1993 by something called the *Vorläufiges Deutsches Biergesetz*—Provisional Beer Laws—additions of beet sugar, pure cane sugar, and invert sugar were made legal in top-fermenting beers, a category which includes the iconic beer style of *hefeweizen*. But the industry has almost universally kept up the old purity routine. And while it's feasible to stay within the *Reinheitsgebot* strictures while trying new combinations and new techniques, most brewers seem to think that following the spirit of the law means you have to brew to some sort of historical flavor archetype. As a result, many modern German brewers shun experimentation of any kind outside of increased mechanical automation. There are only about 20 common styles used for brewing in Germany whereas craft brewers in the United States are working ably in at least 100.

Influencing Attitudes

Another issue is the hypnotic marketing force of *Reinheitsgebot* may make Germans less sophisticated tasters by limiting their perception of what a good beer can be. When asked, many Germans—even well-traveled beer-industry professionals—tend to wrinkle their noses at beers of foreign style or origin. They would sooner drink cheap *biermischgetränke* or mass-produced domestic beers mocked as spülwasser (dishwater) than try anything exotic, such as Belgian ales spiced with herbs or the sort of hoppy, aromatic ales and lagers making waves in the American craft-beer market. If Germans want the taste of something new and exciting, they look to other forms of alcohol.

One exception are the cheap *biermischgetränke* ("beer-mix") products such as *radler* (light beer mixed with lemon-

The Fate of the Reinheitsgebot

International trade and the global economy have finally—after almost 500 years—got the better of the Reinheitsgebot. To the dismay of German brewers, the Reinheitsgebot, with its narrow selection of ingredients, was struck down by the European Court in 1987—as a restraint of free trade. The restrictions it contained were held not permissible in the newly integrated European market.

After centuries of ensuring beer quality, the Reinheitsgebot, therefore, fell victim to the triumph of form over substance. Since the ruling, it has been legal to import beers into Germany that are brewed with adjuncts (corn, rice, non-malted grains and sugar) and treated with chemicals for an artificial head and a longer shelf life. German brewers, however, still adhere fiercely to the Reinheitsgebot as a matter of pride and tradition. German beer labels and advertisements still proudly proclaim the purity of the local brew, and many a German imbiber would not think of letting anything but a "pure" beer pass his or her lips.

"German Beer Primer for Beginners,"
German Beer Institute, 2008. www.germanbeerinstitute.com.

ade, based on an old Munich-area cyclists' tradition), or beer mixed with cola, fruit juice, and other nonalcoholic drinks, which spiked in consumption to a share of 4 percent of the total beer market in 2010—a jump up from 2.7 percent in the previous year. These are considered acceptable innovations because producers claim to "brew first, mix after", thus preserving the tradition of *Reinheitsgebot*. In other words, in today's Germany, it's OK to sell an industrial pilsner mixed with corn-syrupy lemonade or cola flavorings (the latter is called a *diesel*), but the concept of carefully *brewing* a beer with the natural ingredients used in cola—lime, vanilla, coriander, orange peel, and caramel, for starters—remains far-fetched.

As young German consumers have rushed to embrace the latest international wines, cocktails, spirits, alco-pops, mixed drinks, and energy drinks, brewing companies have found themselves saddled with costly excess capacity, forcing them into slimmer profit margins, price wars, mergers and consolidation, and closures.

Signs of Innovation

Despite all these bleak indicators, there's a chance the *brauereisterben* will yield a *brau*-renaissance. Garrett Oliver, of the Brooklyn Brewery, who has brewed considerable quantities of beer with Belgian candy sugar, Sauvignon Blanc lees, exotic botanicals, espresso, even bacon—all to very palatable effects—says he sees signs that German culture is changing, that German brewers and drinkers alike are on the cusp of accepting modern styles.

Starting in 2007, Oliver began collaborating with German brewmaster Hans-Peter Drexler of Schneider (a famous *Reinheitsgebot*-loyal Bavarian brewery that opened in 1872) on a pair of brews, including a strong German *weizenbock* dry-hopped with American flowers. The beer was highly rated, especially in the United States, and the reception in Germany was more or less kind, though the brew wasn't made widely available. "At first I think they were like, 'Oh look, the American has come to learn how to brew from our great brewers,'" recalls Oliver. But the experiment has had a positive ripple effect. Drexler and Oliver's second joint effort (a *hefeweizen*, or traditional Bavarian unfiltered wheat beer) was also dry-hopped with local German Saphir hops from Kelheim post-fermentation, imparting floral and citrusy aromas and flavors practically alien to local palates. The beer remains in Schneider's lineup, and Oliver has been contacted by other

German breweries wanting partnerships. Schneider, too, advertised its eagerness to embark on new collaborations outside Germany.

Even without American assistance, Germans are pushing the hops envelope. Wernecker Bierbrauerei in Werneck, Germany (some 40 miles west of Bamberg), released *Hopfen-Fluch* in 2010, a hoppy, American-style riff on the IPA (India pale ale). Wernecker brewery claims it has doubled in size over the last decade or so, and that sales accelerated 20 percent in 2007, bucking the bleak national trends.

Innovation is happening, if slowly, but German brewers and the drinking public will need to truly embrace change to get the country out of its rut.

Other Collaborations and Experimentation

Hopfen-Fluch and the Oliver-Schneider collaboration beers would likely pass muster under the *Reinheitsgebot*, but change could come with or without the purity business in tow. In Bamberg, Weyermann [Specialty Malts] supplies specialty roasted grains in 80 varieties for the global craft-brewing industry. The company's small, pilot brewery has turned out cherry and pumpkin ales (definitely not *Reinheitsgebot* approved) as well as barley wines (strong English ales) and even "imperial" American-style ales (which might pass inspections, if they existed, depending on carbonation and clarifying methods), all with the intention of "showing the world, and German brewers, what is possible," says Sabine Weyermann, spokesperson for the 130-year-old family-held firm. The Weyermann family sees the *Reinheitsgebot* as less of a "straitjacket" than some believe it to be, because German brewers (with their excess capacity and ingredients on hand) can easily have it both ways—brewing new, rule-breaking beers *and* familiar recipes.

Gasthaus-Brauerei Braustelle in Cologne, a nano-brewery that opened in 2002, is also defying national and local traditions with increasing *chutzpah*: Braumeister Peter Esser's latest beers include a *dunkel* (dark) seasoned with rosemary, an American-style IPA (called Fritz IPA), a 5.8 percent ale infused with hibiscus flowers (Pink Panther) and what's thought to be the first American-style imperial stout ever brewed in Germany (Freigeist Caulfield).

Innovation is happening. If slowly, but German brewers and the drinking public will need to truly embrace change to get the country out of its rut. Blind adherence to a centuries-old edict isn't working anymore. The crucibles of great brewing traditions should be preserved, by all means, and the classic beer recipes and brands along with them—but there can be no doubt: It's time for new blood in the kettles.

An American Brewery Is Resurrecting Ancient Brews

Mark Dredge

Mark Dredge is a staff writer for the Guardian. *In the following viewpoint, he chronicles the trend of rediscovering ingredients used in ancient beers through the practice of molecular archaeology. Brewers are now able to reconstruct these historic beers and create their own recipes using ancient ingredients like yarrow, bog myrtle, and mugwort. Dredge asserts that it is important to keep these ancient traditions alive.*

As you read, consider the following questions:

1. How long does the author say that brewing beer has been around?
2. According to the author, what were the most common ingredients in beer before the discovery of hops?
3. What kinds of fruits does the author say are used in beer?

Give or take a millennium, brewing has been with us for the last 10,000 years. Grain, water, and yeast have been ever present (although before [French microbiologist Louis] Pasteur the yeast was a bit of a mystery), while the practice of adding hops for bitterness in beer has only been in general worldwide use for about 600 years. I've often wondered what

Mark Dredge, "The Beer of Yesteryear," Guardian.co.uk, October 27, 2010. Reprinted by permission.

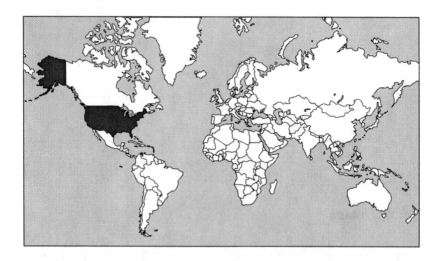

the beers of 500 and 5,000 years ago tasted like, and now, with brewers looking to historic recipes and unfashionable ingredients for inspiration, it's becoming possible to find out.

Beers have, historically, been made with "the indigenous, natural ingredients at hand. The artistry, creativity and diversity of these beers were as colourful and contrasting as the varied cultures in which they were brewed." So say Dogfish Head, a brewery in Milton, Delaware, who have a range of ancient ales formulated by Dr Patrick McGovern, a molecular archaeologist.

Rediscovering Ancient Ingredients

Their Chateau Jiahu is based on evidence from a 9,000-year-old tomb in China, one of the earliest recorded finds of "beer". The Dogfish recreation contains sake rice, wildflower honey, Muscat grapes, hawthorn fruit and chrysanthemum flowers. Midas Touch contains honey, Muscat grapes and saffron and is based on "an ancient Turkish recipe using the original ingredients from the 2,700-year-old drinking vessels discovered in the tomb of King Midas." Theobroma is based on "chemical analysis of pottery fragments found in Honduras which revealed the earliest known alcoholic chocolate drink used by early civilizations to toast special occasions." It contains Aztec cocoa powder and cocoa nibs, honey, chillies and annatto.

Our ancestors would quickly have discovered that you can't consume a sweet drink in any real quantity, and as their taste for the intoxicating effects of alcohol grew, the hunt for bittering ingredients to make beer a thirst-quenching experience began. Before hops, brewers would add a wide variety of locally available herbs and plants to their beers; the most common ingredients were bog myrtle and yarrow but others included:

> "sage, wormwood, rosemary, broom (very popular), dandelions, nettles . . . alehoof . . . wood avens or herb bennet," explains brewing historian Martyn Cornell. "Beyond these, heather, ground ivy, juniper, wild carrot seed, poppy, various spices and pepper were all used."

Gruit is a style which predates the use of hops, the name referring to the mixture of herbs used. Stuart Howe at Sharp's Brewery brewed a gruit earlier this year [2010] containing yarrow, turmeric, bay and lemon balm. Moonlight Brewing in California brewed Artemis, a gruit containing mugwort and wild bergamot.

Away from liquid time capsules and historical recreations, breweries are experimenting with adding herbs and spices to beers with increasing regularity.

More Recently Revived Styles

Sahti is a traditional Finnish beer style which is filtered through juniper twigs and fermented with bakers' yeast. Nøgne Ø, a Norwegian brewery, make a sahti with sea wormwood, juniper, heather honey, three yeasts plus hops and a variety of grains. Another recently revived style is purl, a beer flavoured with wormwood which may have been served warm with a slug of gin; Sonoma Springs from California makes Green

Beer and Death

Alcohol may be at the heart of human life, but the bulk of [beer archaeologist Patrick] McGovern's most significant samples come from tombs. Many bygone cultures seem to have viewed death as a last call of sorts, and mourners provisioned the dead with beverages and receptacles—agate drinking horns, straws of lapis lazuli and, in the case of a Celtic woman buried in Burgundy around the sixth century B.C., a 1,200-liter caldron—so they could continue to drink their fill in eternity. King Scorpion I's tomb was flush with once-full wine jars. Later Egyptians simply diagramed beer recipes on the walls so the pharaoh's servants in the afterlife could brew more (presumably freeing up existing beverages for the living).

Some of the departed had festive plans for the afterlife. In 1957, when University of Pennsylvania archaeologists first tunneled into the nearly airtight tomb of King Midas, encased in an earthen mound near Ankara, Turkey, they discovered the body of a 60- to 65-year-old man fabulously arrayed on a bed of purple and blue cloth beside the largest cache of Iron Age drinking paraphernalia ever found: 157 bronze buckets, vats and bowls. And as soon as the archaeologists let fresh air into the vault, the tapestries' vivid colors began fading before their eyes.

Abigail Tucker, "The Beer Archaeologist,"
Smithsonian, August 2011.

Purl which includes wormwood, horseradish, orange peel and juniper in a dry and herbal brew with an intense tonsil-beating botanical finish.

Williams Bros Brewery in Alloa, Scotland, produces a range of historic ales alongside their contemporary range. Their most popular historic ale is Froach, made with heather and sweet gale making for a floral, spicy and perfumed pint. Their Grozet ale includes bog myrtle, meadow sweet and gooseberries; Alba includes pine and spruce sprigs; and Kelpie includes seaweed which adds a distinct peppery, vegetal quality which works very well with the rich, roasty base beer.

Welcome Innovations

So where is this newfound enthusiasm for ancient ingredients leading brewers? Away from liquid time capsules and historical recreations, breweries are experimenting with adding herbs and spices to beers with increasing regularity. Ginger is popular, making for genuine ginger ales, adding fragrant, warming spice; elderflower creates a floral, fruity flavour—Thornbridge's Craven Silk is a fine example; Dogfish Head, Stone Brewing and Victory Brewing have Saison du BUFF, a three-way collaboration which has a recipe inclined towards Mediterranean food and includes parsley, sage, rosemary and thyme; Vapeur brewery's Saison de Pipaix contains black pepper, ginger, orange peel, curaçao and star anise, and their other beers include cumin, coriander and vanilla; Hugh Fearnley-Whittingstall and Badger Brewery have created River Cottage Stinger made with nettles which add a grassy, herbal flavour.

Badger also makes a beer with dandelion and while not added for bitterness, fruit is a traditional beer ingredient, particularly in Belgium, and there is evidence of fruit beer being on sale in London in the 1700s—the most popular and frequently used today are cherries, raspberries, blueberries, strawberries and apricots; other ingredients you may see around include juniper, clove, peppercorns, liquorice, hibiscus, tea, chamomile and spruce.

Unusual or not, there's a long history of beers brewed with a wealth of ingredients, be they fruits, spices, herbs or hops. Now, as brewers look to their forebears for inspiration, beers with these flavours are available to the modern drinker and keeping the traditions alive. What do you think: wormwood in your beer? Stinging nettles or seaweed? Does yarrow, sage and bog myrtle sound appetising?

Periodical and Internet Sources Bibliography

The following articles have been selected to supplement the diverse views presented in this chapter.

Michael Apstein	"Wine Culture Starting to Take Hold in China," *San Francisco Chronicle*, May 8, 2011.
Hannah Aronowitz	"Microbreweries Serve Up Alternative Beer Culture in Medellin," Colombia Reports, March 30, 2011. http://colombiareports.com.
Jason Clenfield	"Nakagawa's Exit Highlights Japan's Alcohol-Fueled Work Culture," Bloomberg.com, March 4, 2009. www.bloomberg.com.
Economist	"Pub Culture and Pub Economy," November 30, 2010.
Colby Gergen	"Chug, Chug, Chug: Our Culture of Binge Drinking," The Next Great Generation, July 26, 2010. www.thenextgreatgeneration.com.
Aimee Groth	"Binge Drinking Is Becoming a Requirement for Chinese Execs," Business Insider, August 23, 2011. www.businessinsider.com.
Mitch Moxley	"Binge-Drinking Culture Turning from Fun to Lethal," Inter Press Service, March 12, 2010. http://ipsnews.net.
Mary Orlin	"Birth of a Wine Culture in America," *Huffington Post*, March 30, 2011. www.huffingtonpost.com.
Josh Rubin	"Wine Laws Can Drive You to Despair," *Toronto Star*, May 27, 2011.
Kate Torgovnick	"Girl Talk: Why Being Drunk Is a Feminist Issue," TheFrisky.com, June 1, 2011. www.thefrisky.com.

For Further Discussion

Chapter 1

1. This chapter explores some of the global trends in alcohol consumption. After reading the viewpoints in the chapter, which trend do you find the most troubling? Have you seen any of these trends in your community? Provide details.

2. In his viewpoint, Christopher Sopher juxtaposes European youth drinking culture with American youth drinking culture. How is the way young Europeans drink changing? Are European authorities right to be concerned? Explain your answer.

Chapter 2

1. John M. McCardell Jr. argues in his viewpoint that the United States should lower its drinking age. Is his argument persuasive? Do you disagree or agree with his perspective? Explain your reasoning.

2. This chapter discusses a number of strategies governments and policy makers are considering to address the problem of alcoholism and alcohol-related violence. Which do you believe are the most promising? Which do you think are the least effective? Explain your answer.

Chapter 3

1. In his viewpoint, Alexander Smoltczyk reports on how the Muslim country of Qatar is handling the issue of alcohol sales and consumption for the 2022 World Cup. In your opinion, how well is Qatar dealing with the situation? What else could Qatar do to accommodate World Cup fans?

2. The viewpoints in this chapter explore the way Muslim countries treat the issue of alcohol. What kind of problems are the Muslim prohibitions on alcohol causing for these countries? How can these problems be addressed?

Chapter 4

1. Britain has had much success with its Campaign for Real Ale. What are the advantages of emphasizing a traditional drinking culture in Britain? What will be the social and economic benefits of a successful campaign? Explain your answer.

2. This chapter surveys different alcohol and drinking cultures around the world. What is the alcohol culture in your community? What are the strong points of your community's alcohol culture? The weak points? Provide details.

Organizations to Contact

The editors have compiled the following list of organizations concerned with the issues debated in this book. The descriptions are derived from materials provided by the organizations. All have publications or information available for interested readers. The list was compiled on the date of publication of the present volume; the information provided here may change. Be aware that many organizations take several weeks or longer to respond to inquiries, so allow as much time as possible.

ABMRF/The Foundation for Alcohol Research
1122 Kenilworth Drive, Suite 407, Baltimore, MD   21204
(410) 821-7066 • fax: (410) 821-7065
e-mail: info@abmrf.org
website: www.abmrf.org

ABMRF/The Foundation for Alcohol Research is an independent, nonprofit foundation in North America that conducts and supports biomedical, behavioral, and social science research on alcohol consumption and alcohol abuse. The foundation investigates the factors influencing drinking behavior; assesses the health issues associated with alcohol consumption; and researches the efficacy of various alcohol abuse prevention strategies. Much of this research can be accessed on its website, which also features news, listings of recent events, and information on the grant process.

Alcoholics Anonymous (AA)
PO Box 459, New York, NY   10163
(212) 870-3400
e-mail: international@aa.org
website: www.aa.org

Alcoholics Anonymous (AA) is an international organization that provides a forum for alcoholics to come together to facilitate and support the recovery process. Over the years, AA has developed treatment tools like AA's Twelve Steps of spiritual and character development and the Twelve Traditions to aid in recovery. AA is based on local and regional groups that are economically self-sustaining and emphasize confidentiality when it comes to the identity of its participants. AA publishes several pamphlets, brochures, reports, and books, as well as a periodical known as the *AA Grapevine*, which covers recent news, updates on new treatments and therapies, and events.

American Beverage Institute (ABI)

1090 Vermont Avenue NW, Suite 800, Washington, DC   20005
(202) 463-7110
website: www.abionline.org

The American Beverage Institute (ABI) was founded in 1991 as a restaurant trade association formed to protect the rights of consumers to drink alcohol responsibly. It often works against anti-alcohol groups that strive to eliminate or restrict alcohol from public places. ABI represents the biggest restaurant chains in the United States as well as individual restaurants and other hospitality businesses. One of ABI's key tools in this mission is research, which it sponsors and then utilizes to lobby legislators and policy makers. The ABI website features the latest news in the industry, updates on legislative efforts, and commentary.

Brewers Association

PO 1679, Boulder, CO   80306
(303) 447-0816
e-mail: info@brewersassociation.org
website: www.brewersassociation.org

The Brewers Association is an organization of American brewers, wholesalers, and members of associated trades. It describes its mission as the promotion and protection of small and independent American brewers and the brewing community. The Brewers Association is particularly active on policy and legislative issues, working to craft and support laws and regulations that help the American brewing industry. The

Brewers Association website features a blog, links to recent news and information on events, and videos. It also publishes the *New Brewer*, a bimonthly periodical that examines industry issues, as well as guides and manuals for brewing beginners.

Campaign for Real Ale (CAMRA)

230 Hatfield Road, St. Albans   AL1 4LW
  England
01727 867 201
e-mail: camra@camra.org.uk
website: www.camra.org.uk

The Campaign for Real Ale (CAMRA) is a European-based campaign to promote traditional ales, ciders, and perries, as well as celebrate the role of the public house in community life. CAMRA is a voluntary organization and consumer group that emphasizes quality, consumer value, community, and heritage. The CAMRA website features information on festivals, promotions, and events; hosts a beer video blog; offers discounts and beer guides; provides a monthly e-newsletter called the *Campaigner*; and includes an online bookstore. CAMRA also publishes a newspaper, *What's Brewing*, and a periodical, *Beer*, both of which can be accessed on the campaign's website.

European Alcohol Policy Alliance

96, Rue des Confédérés, Brussels   B-1000
  Belgium
+32 2 736 05 72
e-mail: info@eurocare.org
website: www.eurocare.org

The European Alcohol Policy Alliance, also known as Eurocare, is an alliance of public health organizations from twenty-two European countries working to prevent and reduce the negative public health and safety consequences of alcohol consumption. According to its website, "[m]ember organisations are involved in research and advocacy, as well as in the provision of counseling services and residential support for problem drinkers, the provision of workplace and school-based programmes and the provision of information to the public." The website also includes information on the latest campaigns and projects and offers access to recent reports, statistical research, news, and the alliance's monthly newsletter.

Institute of Alcohol Studies (IAS)

Alliance House, 12 Caxton Street, London   SW1H 0QS
+44 (0) 207 222 4001 • fax: +44 (0) 207 799 2510
e-mail: info@ias.org.uk
website: www.ias.org.uk

The Institute of Alcohol Studies (IAS) works to provide an independent voice on alcohol policy. Because IAS is not funded by the government nor by the alcohol industry, it can objectively analyze scientific research on drinking and alcohol abuse policy in order to formulate and lobby for sound public health policy on alcohol and drinking. IAS is known for its well-respected reports and studies by experts in the field as well as its exhaustive study *Alcohol in Europe*. It also publishes a quarterly magazine, *Alcohol Alert*, which explores issues of interest in the industry. *Alcohol Alert* is accessible on the IAS website.

International Center for Alcohol Policies (ICAP)

1519 New Hampshire Avenue NW, Washington, DC   20036
(202) 986-1159 • fax: (202) 986-2080
e-mail: info@icap.org
website: www.icap.org

The International Center for Alcohol Policies (ICAP) is a nonprofit group funded by the alcohol industry that works to protect the interests of beverage manufacturers and consumers and combat and prevent alcohol abuse. ICAP is also tasked with facilitating dialogue and forming partnerships between governments and policy makers; the alcohol, retail, and hospitality industry; and the public health community. ICAP offers a wide range of publications, including meeting reports, studies, and research; books on preventing alcohol abuse and how the industry can more effectively combat the problem; the *ICAP Periodical Review on Drinking and Culture*, an e-publication that offers English translations of the latest research on alcohol addiction and the alcohol industry; and other publications on international alcohol policy.

Mothers Against Drunk Driving (MADD)

511 E. John Carpenter Freeway, Suite 700, Irving, TX   75062
(877) 275-6233 • fax: (972) 869-2206
website: www.madd.org

Mothers Against Drunk Driving (MADD) is a nonprofit organization that was created to support families and communities affected by drunk driving. MADD advocates for stronger legislation and penalties against drunk driving and formulates policies to fight underage drinking. MADD has proposed, for example, that all cars be installed with a breath alcohol ignition device that would prevent a car from starting if the driver is over the legal blood alcohol level. The MADD website offers access to the organization's monthly newsletter, *MADD Messenger*, and its biannual periodical, *MADDvocate*.

National Institute on Alcohol Abuse and Alcoholism (NIAAA)

5635 Fishers Lane, MSC 9304, Bethesda, MD   20892-9304
(301) 443-3860
website: www.niaaa.nih.gov

The National Institute on Alcohol Abuse and Alcoholism (NIAAA) is a division of the National Institutes of Health and states its mission as conducting and supporting alcohol-related research in a range of scientific fields, including genetics, neuroscience, and epidemiology; coordinating research and policy with other research institutes and federal bureaus; collaborating with international, state, regional, and state governments; and disseminating relevant research to policy makers, the health care industry, and the public. The NIAAA website features news, listings of events, congressional testimony, guidelines and educational material, studies, and in-depth research on alcohol-related topics. The NIAAA also publishes a quarterly newsletter, the *NIAAA Newsletter*, which reports on the agency's activities and recent events, and a quarterly bulletin, *Alcohol Alert*, which disseminates research findings on a single aspect of alcohol abuse and alcoholism.

World Health Organization (WHO)

Avenue Appia 20, Geneva 27   1211
   Switzerland
(+41) 22 791 21 11 • fax: (+41) 22 791 31 11
e-mail: info@who.int
website: www.who.int

The World Health Organization (WHO) is the United Nations agency responsible for directing global health care matters. WHO funds research on health issues that affect global health, including the problem of alcoholism. The agency monitors health trends, compiles useful statistics, and offers technical support to countries dealing with the consequences of alcohol abuse. The WHO website features podcasts, blogs, and videos; it also offers fact sheets, reports, studies, and a calendar of events.

Bibliography of Books

Charles W.
Bamforth

Beer Is Proof God Loves Us: Reaching for the Soul of Beer and Brewing. Upper Saddle River, NJ: FT Press, 2011.

Gina Barreca, ed.

Make Mine a Double: Why Women Like Us Like to Drink (or Not). Hanover, NH: University Press of New England, 2011.

Joshua M.
Bernstein

Brewed Awakening: Behind the Beers and Brewers Leading the World's Craft Brewing Revolution. New York: Sterling, 2011.

Pete Brown

Three Sheets to the Wind: One Man's Quest for the Meaning of Beer. London: Pan, 2007.

Ian Buxton

The Enduring Legacy of Dewars: A Company History. Glasgow, UK: Angels' Share, 2009.

Steve Charters,
ed.

The Business of Champagne. New York: Routledge, 2012.

Diane Kirkby,
Tanja Luckins,
and Chris
McConville

The Australian Pub. Sydney: University of New South Wales Press, 2010.

Todd Kliman

The Wild Vine: A Forgotten Grape and the Untold Story of American Wine. New York: Clarkson Potter, 2010.

Greg Koch and Matt Allyn — *The Brewer's Apprentice: An Insider's Guide to the Art and Craft of Beer Brewing, Taught by the Masters.* Beverly, MA: Quarry Books, 2011.

Li Zhengping — *Chinese Wine.* Cambridge, UK: Cambridge University Press, 2011.

Jeffrey V. Maars, ed. — *Alcohol Dependence and Addiction.* Hauppauge, NY: Nova Science, 2011.

Hal Marcovitz — *Should the Drinking Age Be Lowered?* San Diego: ReferencePoint Press, 2011.

Amy Mittelman — *Brewing Battles: The History of American Beer.* New York: Algora Publishing, 2007.

Randy Mosher — *Tasting Beer: An Insider's Guide to the World's Greatest Drink.* North Adams, MA: Storey Publishing, 2009.

James Nicholls — *Politics of Alcohol: A History of the Drink Question in England.* Manchester, UK: Manchester University Press, 2009.

Richard Paterson and Gavin D. Smith — *Goodness Nose: The Passionate Revelations of a Scotch Whiskey Master Blender.* Glasgow, UK: Angels' Share, 2010.

Thomas Pellechia — *Wine: The 8,000-Year-Old Story of the Wine Trade.* New York: Thunder's Mouth Press, 2006.

Thomas Pinney   *The Makers of American Wine: A Record of Two Hundred Years.* Berkeley: University of California Press, 2012.

Erica Prussing   *White Man's Water: The Politics of Sobriety in a Native American Community.* Tucson: University of Arizona Press, 2011.

Anne Rooney   *Alcohol.* Mankato, MN: Arcturus, 2011.

Harvey Sawler   *Last Canadian Beer: The Moosehead Story.* Halifax, Nova Scotia: Nimbus Publishing, 2008.

James Simpson   *Creating Wine: The Emergence of a World Industry, 1840–1914.* Princeton, NJ: Princeton University Press, 2011.

Robert W. Small   *Beverage Basics: Understanding and Appreciating Wine, Beer, and Spirits.* Hoboken, NJ: Wiley, 2011.

Robert W. Small and Michelle Couturier   *Wine, Beers, and Spirits.* Hoboken, NJ: Wiley, 2011.

Clive Tobutt, ed.   *Alcohol at Work: Managing Alcohol Problems and Issues in the Workplace.* Burlington, VT: Gower, 2011.

Jerome Tuccille   *Gallo Be Thy Name: The Inside Story of How One Family Rose to Dominate the US Wine Market.* Beverly Hills, CA: Phoenix Books, 2009.

Thomas Vander Ven — *Getting Wasted: Why College Students Drink Too Much and Party So Hard.* New York: New York University Press, 2011.

James Waller — *Drinkology Beer: A Book About the Brew.* New York: Stewart, Tabori & Chang, 2011.

Brian Yaeger — *Red, White, and Brew: An American Beer Odyssey.* New York: St. Martin's Griffin, 2008.

Index

Geographic headings and page numbers in **boldface** refer to viewpoints about that country or region.